MORE PRAISE FOR

Bearing the Unbearable

"A truly remarkable book."

—ROBERT D. STOLOROW, author of *Trauma and Human Existence*

"An approach to grief that moves beyond platitudes and cliché. It offers a way to truly grow through grief that is not a moving beyond but is more of an organic composting and recycling of the soul. It offers hope for those who feel like their loss has disconnected themselves forever from humanity and the circle of life. There is something for everyone in this garden that will restore and rejuvenate."

—DOUG BREMNER, MD, professor of psychiatry at Emory University and author of *The Goose That Laid the Golden Egg*

"*Bearing the Unbearable* is an experience more than a book. It shows us—through its many emotionally gripping examples guaranteed to trigger readers' own lurking tears—much that is novel and illuminating about the ineffable depth and labyrinthine nature of intense grief."

—JEROME WAKEFIELD, DSW, PHD, professor, NYU School of Medicine and author of *The Loss of Sadness*

"An honest and courageous examination of the most common of human experiences. Dr. Cacciatore's powerful book shows grieving human beings how to reclaim the process as normal and sacred, and how to insist on defining the process for themselves—which leads to healing."

—MARY NEAL VIETEN, PHD, ABPP, Executive Director, Warfighter Advance

Bearing
the Unbearable

LOVE, LOSS, AND THE
HEARTBREAKING PATH OF GRIEF

Joanne Cacciatore, PhD

Foreword by Jeffrey B. Rubin, PhD

Wisdom Publications
132 Perry Street
New York, NY 10014 USA
wisdomexperience.org

Library of Congress Cataloging-in-Publication Data
Names: Cacciatore, Joanne, author.
Title: Bearing the unbearable: love, loss, and the heartbreaking path of grief / Joanne
     Cacciatore.
Description: Somerville, MA: Wisdom Publications, [2017] | Includes index.
Identifiers: LCCN 2016044492 (print) | LCCN 2017000554 (ebook) | ISBN 9781614292968
     (pbk.: alk. paper) | ISBN 1614292965 (pbk.: alk. paper) | ISBN 9781614293170 (ebook) |
     ISBN 1614293171 (ebook)
Subjects: LCSH: Grief. | Loss (Psychology) | Adjustment (Psychology) | Love.
Classification: LCC BF575.G7 C27 2017 (print) | LCC BF575.G7 (ebook) | DDC
     155.9/37—dc23
LC record available at https://lccn.loc.gov/2016044492

ISBN 978-1-61429-296-8   ebook ISBN 978-1-61429-317-0

23
8

Cover design by Jim Zaccaria.
Interior design by Gopa&Ted2. Set in Granjon LT Std 11.5/15.9.

Wisdom Publications' books are printed on acid-free paper and meet
the guidelines for permanence and durability of the Production Guidelines
for Book Longevity of the Council on Library Resources.

Printed in the United States of America.

Please visit fscus.org.

In eternal homage to our beloved dead.

*And for all the mourners who have entrusted me
to be companion to them amid their utmost
uninhabitable hollows of grief.*

*For my four who walk
And for Cheyenne,
my one who soars:*

Then, now, always, for kalpas.

Grief comes to one and all; no one is exempt.

We must remember our dead.

We must do better for the bereaved.

We must embody compassion.

To be redeemed we must remember.

Remembering is our duty—

and the only thing that will save us.

Contents

List of Grieving Practices Mentioned

Foreword

BY JEFFREY B. RUBIN

We live in a precarious world in which loss and grief assail us at a seemingly ever-quickening pace.

In a culture like our own that is addicted to the relentless quest to feel happy—perhaps as an unconscious attempt to bypass our disavowed misery—grief is taboo, pathologized, and aggressively avoided. Grievers are advised to "look on the bright side," "think positive," and "count your blessings." When such empty platitudes don't work—basically always—people who experience anguish may often be numbed with drugs. And this leaves victims of loss and grief guilty or shame-ridden about their sadness and without the resources to handle their pain. What's crucial in trauma—and what makes it bearable (as psychoanalyst Robert Stolorow usefully reminds us in *Trauma and Human Existence*) is having an emotional home for our feelings. Grief that is dismissed, suppressed, or silenced harms individuals, families, and communities. It leads, as Dr. Joanne Cacciatore aptly notes in this wonderful book, to "addictions, abuse, and violence, often against the vulnerable: children, women, elderly, and animals."

In *Bearing the Unbearable*, Dr. Cacciatore, an associate professor at Arizona State University, an expert in traumatic loss and grief, a Zen priest, and herself a bereaved mother, shows us a healthier path. Drawing on more than two decades of clinical experience; research findings; the wisdom of Buddhist, Christian, Jewish, and Native American sages; and Western psychology, Dr. Cacciatore illuminates the emotional impact of grief and the psychological, relational, and spiritual elements of healing and transformation. This moving and insightful book is a superb counterweight to the mad rush in our grief-averse culture to deny negative feelings and anesthetize emotional anguish.

In poignant chapters on such topics as the cost of unrealized and unprocessed grief and trauma, transgenerational grief, guilt and shame, the relationship of loss and love, the practice of being with grief, and the value of rituals and micro-rituals, she clarifies not only the strategies individuals and the medical and psychiatric establishment use to deny, suppress, and anesthetize grief and mourning, but also the pathway to healing. *Bearing the Unbearable* offers a compelling critique of our "compassion-deficient" and happiness-addicted culture that creates a pathological relationship to our feelings in general and grief in particular. Dr. Cacciatore elucidates the cost of pathologizing grief and neglecting and invalidating the emotional experience of people who have suffered horrendous loss—the way such approaches make the grief-stricken doubt themselves and feel alienated and isolated—all of which precludes healing.

This book makes a plea for therapeutic approaches to trauma and grief that unflinchingly respect the full spectrum of feelings that human beings experience, thus providing an emotional home for our agony. Drawing on touching and sometimes heart-wrenching stories from her practice and her life, Dr. Joanne Cacciatore—lovingly known to tens of thousands of grief-stricken people she has worked with on six continents as "Jojo"—demonstrates what is necessary to facilitate healing. With searing honesty, inspiring courage, and exemplary empathy, Dr. Cacciatore greets the agony of her clients with patience and compassion and an intrepid spirit of curiosity and patience. And readers may feel themselves subtly transformed.

Bearing the Unbearable not only offers tales of remarkable healing; it is also an astonishing testament to the mysterious and transformational power of grief that is met with compassion to grow our heart, expand our circle of compassion, and generate lives of greater meaning. The traumatized live in a different psychological universe than the untraumatized. Ripped open by loss and grief, the former can also awake from the consensual trance of everyday life. Dr. Cacciatore elucidates two ways this can be transformative—heightened gratitude and what she calls "fierce compassion." "No one is as capable of gratitude as one who has emerged from the kingdom of night," the late Elie Wiesel recognized. In Dr. Cacciatore's book we are exposed to people who suffered traumatic grief and then teach us about expanded gratitude and service to others. "Fierce compassion," which arises from fully experienced grief, helps us awake from our slumber and live more wholeheartedly. It helps us take more responsibility for reaching beyond ourselves and toward other people and the suffering that is haunting them. Dr. Cacciatore believes that it is a force that can heal the world.

Bearing the Unbearable is filled with heartwarming stories and original insights; it shows that pain can be a doorway into wisdom and fierce compassion. Dr. Cacciatore convinces us that we have to *do with* grief as well as *be with* it. This book will expand your mind, warm your heart, and enrich your spirit. *Bearing the Unbearable* is not just a critique of grief-avoidance and a plea for empathy and compassion, but it is also an invitation to a life of openness and care, courage and service.

I wholeheartedly recommended this book to people who have suffered loss, mental health professionals and spiritual seekers, students and teachers in the humanities, as well as ordinary people who yearn to live a life of greater aliveness and fulfillment. After reading Dr. Cacciatore's wonderful book, you will not only hold your own grief and the sadness of other people more skillfully; you will also live and love more wisely.

Dr. Jeffrey B. Rubin is the author of *Psychotherapy and Buddhism: Toward an Integration,* and *The Art of Flourishing: A New East-West Approach to Staying Sane and Finding Love in an Insane World.*

Prologue

Seeking to forget makes exile all the longer;
the secret to redemption lies in remembrance.
—RICHARD VON WEIZSÄCKER

I.

THERE IS A PLACE, an inviolable place, where her name is ensconced, beaten and burned into the deepest crevices of my heart.

It was a hot summer day when I buried my baby daughter, Cheyenne. I watched as the men in gray suits scooped heaps of soft earth atop the pink satin casket that held her wrapped body. It was a small service—there were so few who knew her.

There were no teen friends to bid her farewell and lament her early death. There were no teachers to boast of her goodness. There was no neighbor who had watched her to express how she would miss her smile. There was just me, or so it felt, and my breasts that burned in engorged dissent at her sudden death.

Only hours earlier, I had closed the casket lid myself. There are no words to describe such a physical, emotional, and existential loss other than by saying that I also died with her that day.

I did not ask for this.

I did not want this.

I hated everything about it.

I remember asking how the world could continue spinning after such a tragedy. I wanted to scream at the cars driving past the cemetery. I wanted to yell at the birds in the trees casting shadows on her headstone. I wanted the grass to stop growing and the clouds to stop floating and the other children, now being buried there, to stop dying.

As the hours turned to days and the days to weeks, my grief intensified, stretching every plane of my being. It felt like a physical dying, repeated every day upon the opening of my eyes on the rare occasions that sleep had actually come. Breathing hurt, and a global pain emanated from the tips of my hair to the tips of my toes.

I paced the hallways late at night like a caged wild animal—searching for my baby.

Her body was gone, but every part of me was evolutionarily programmed to be with her, to feed her from my breast, to comfort her cries, to touch her skin. The pangs of longing were insatiable, maddening, and at many times I questioned my own lucidity. What I didn't know was that I was changing, being agonizingly transformed—but knowing that wouldn't have eased the pain even one little bit.

And to this day, I'd gladly give it all back to have her here . . .

WHEN A PERSON BELOVED BY US DIES, our lives can become unbearable.

And yet we are asked—by life, by death—to bear it, to suffer the insufferable, to endure the unendurable. *Bearing the Unbearable* is an expression of my own heart and my life's work—demanding and formidable, satisfying and deeply vital.

This book will not offer you a spiritual bypass; it won't make it so you don't have to face the pain of grief—nor should it. When we love deeply, we mourn deeply; extraordinary grief is an expression of extraordinary love. Grief and love mirror each other; one is not possible without the other.

What this book will do, I hope, is to provide a safe space to *feel*, to be with your understandably broken heart. It will serve as an invitation to stay with the wretched pangs of sorrow, to dwell in the dark night of your own bereaved soul, and to be present with what is—however difficult, however painful.

The word *bereave* derives from an Old English word, *befearfian*, meaning "to deprive, take away, or be robbed," and when death robs us, our mourning, our loss, resonates through time. We mourn for tomorrow's moments, and next month's moments, and next year's moments; we mourn at the graduations and weddings, the births, and the deaths that follow. Grief consists of countless particles, countless moments, each one of which can be mourned. And through them all, we always know in our very cells that someone is missing, that there is a place in our hearts that can never be filled.

With a loved one's death, the person we once were evaporates, and we take on what may feel like an aberrant form of ourselves, an unfamiliar way of being in the world. This is not what we wanted, this is not what we planned, this is not what *should* be—but it is what we have—even as our heart whispers, *"No, no, no."* And here we find ourselves, feeling outcast, lying face down on the ground or on bent and bloodied knee or with our arms outstretched, pleading for relief.

Death feels savage, and to some extent, it is—but grief need not be vilified.

We might never accept that our child or parent or spouse or grandchild or friend or loved one has died, but we can learn to accept how we *feel* about that loss, where in us the pain is most acute, its dimensions and texture, its tenor and depth. And over time, grief can morph from a dreaded, unwanted intruder to something more familiar and less terrifying—a companion, perhaps.

Make no mistake: losing someone we love deeply changes us, inescapably and for all time, and it is painful beyond all imagining. The psychologist Rollo May wrote, "One does not become fully human painlessly." It is through inhabiting, often painfully, our emotions that we are able to become fully human. Through grief, we can experience an alchemical transformation that cannot be contrived, hastened, or imparted by others.

To fully inhabit grief is to hold the contradictions of the great mystery that loss shatters us and we become whole. Grief empties us and we are filled with emotion. Fear paralyzes us and we lend courage to another. We mourn our beloveds' absence and we invoke their presence. We cease to exist as we once were and we become more fully human. We know the darkest of all nights and in so doing can bring the light of our loved ones into the world.

We are the paradox.

We are the bearers of the unbearable.

II.

THE HEART OF THIS BOOK began with my daughter's death, but the writing of it started on a six-week East Coast speaking tour. My experiences on that trip, especially on the long train ride back, served to underscore for me yet again just how important and powerful attending to grief truly is.

On this trip, I'd traveled first to Richmond, Virginia, where I'd taught grief-focused meditation. Attendees had cried quietly in the space we had all created—and I was reminded of the words of Ajahn Chah: "Unless one has deeply wept, one has not yet begun to meditate." We'd lit candles, and we'd remembered. We'd held each other. Some had lost loved ones just weeks prior to the workshop, others decades earlier.

I'd traveled to the Bacon family home in Newtown, Connecticut, and stepped down the same wooden floors that first-grader Charlotte Helen Bacon had walked before the tragic mass shooting at Sandy Hook Elementary School. I'd met her brother, and he autographed a copy of the book he'd written to honor his murdered little sister. Her parents and I had visited the place where she is buried, near her friends, and we'd stood in silence. What is there to say in the presence of unspeakable tragedy?

I'd traveled to New York, where I'd guided health care providers in listening to others' grief, layer upon layer. For four consecutive days, those usually tasked with helping others had reconnected with their own soul wounds. For some, latent grief was like a faded photograph whose edges had frayed from years of handling—and, like their clients, they too needed a safe place to revisit ancient injuries.

At that conference, a panel of grieving mothers had reflected on their experiences of loss and shared the ways they remembered their children through their own ongoing lives of service—and those little ones, those remembered children, became great teachers of compassion for us all. One mother had told us how she had had to be physically restrained after the unexpected death of her baby—and now she helps parents all over the world. Another woman had shared how she grapples with guilt because her actions, albeit inadvertent, had killed her daughter. Now she is studying to become a grief counselor. Another person had described the events that led to the murders of her two young children and talked about the work she now does reaching out to other parents whose children have been murdered.

I heard so many stories of love and loss and grief. Sometimes they were offered boldly in front of groups; sometimes they were hushed confessions in the back of a room. Sometimes people contacted me hours or days later through the comparative safety of email—their stories of grief having burst like a seedling through soil made dense by years of compaction.

And now, boarding the train and heading back home, I reflected on a mysterious quality of grief: when we look into the eyes of another, someone who has known suffering, without a word *we* know that *they* know, and there is something painfully restorative in that mutual recognition.

On the train, again and again, I found conversations that began simply would rapidly become deep, meaningful exchanges about love and loss, about life and death. One young man with calm eyes and a bright smile, recounted watching helplessly as a train struck and killed his friend, noting with obvious sadness that the one-year anniversary of that event was near at hand. After a brief conversation with a young mother and her little boy about the challenges of train travel with toddlers, she asked about what I did for work. I told her, and then she went on to tell me about the death of her oldest brother and how her mother was never the same after losing him—because the family has an unspoken rule not to speak of that boy's death, and thus not to say anything about his life or their love for him.

One morning over breakfast, I sat across from an older man from Southern California who wore a John Deere cap and whose swollen belly rested on the table. We got to talking and at some point he looked up from his Greek yogurt and said, "I know plenty about grief and trauma" and began to speak about his years on a SWAT team. "You wouldn't believe the things I saw," he said—and went on to describe encounters so traumatic they continued to affect him even after thirty-five years. "I was strong, stoic. I never shed a tear, . . . but since I retired, it's like I'm always crying, always emotional." I nodded and it felt appropriate to ask him how long it had been since he had started feeling all this. He paused and looked at the ceiling. "You know, I don't know. I've just never felt so many emotions so deeply. I am starting to wonder if there is something wrong with me." By the end of our conversation, though, he concluded on his own that feeling this onrush of emotion now was "probably normal" because as he said, "back then you weren't allowed to show weakness on the job or cry."

Another man from St. Louis told me over oatmeal one morning about the death of his first wife. He'd left himself little time to grieve and remarried within months because his sadness was "too much to bear alone." Still never having shaken his sorrow, he and his second wife divorced two years later, after the birth of their first child, and he began drinking heavily and lost contact with his only offspring. The pain from all those losses had etched lines on his face.

I met a seventy-eight-year-old retired nurse from Dayton as she was grumbling about Amtrak's limited tea offerings. I told her that I'm a tea snob too and so I carry my own organic blend. I offered her some, and she asked what I was doing on the East Coast. When I told her, she looked down at her cup of steaming Earl Grey. She pursed her lips and took a sip, noticeably uncomfortable, and then let out a protracted sigh. "You know, I had a daughter," she said. "She would be about your age." She sighed again—and then for more than two hours, past mountain ranges, graffitied bridges, and scattered fields of cotton, she shared with me the story of her daughter, who had died in 1974. It was a story she had never told anyone in full. When she was done, she said, "I imagine my daughter would have been such a nice young woman, just like you." We both had tears in our eyes.

My travels eastward and back home seemed to me symbolic of so many journeys through love and grief. Looking out the window by my seat, I saw abandoned playgrounds and decrepit barns juxtaposed with freshly painted schools and flourishing farms. I saw dried up riverbeds and lush riparian bluffs. I saw dying ponds and verdant streams. At times, the ride was turbulent and jarring, and at other times it was placid and smooth.

The train, like grief, had its own rhythm and varying speeds and changing conditions—influenced by weather, good or not-so-good maintenance, and by the terrain over which we traveled. Sometimes we seemed to crawl slowly across the miles—and I could focus on the silos of Garden City or the herd of antelope on the Comanche National Grassland. At other times, high velocity blurred even the most majestic trees, colors blending together, shapes indistinguishable.

There were places on the track where a simple switch could alter our direction; these reminded me of the way in grief we can move toward denial or toward love, toward mourning or disavowal. In tunnels, there were times when it was so dark it was impossible to see any light at all; grief has such times too. My eyes needed time to adjust, but after they had, in those dark places I found I could discern what was there. Sometimes my cell phone had service and sometimes it didn't; sometimes I'd had connection to the outside world and other times I'd been utterly disconnected—just as with grieving.

Looking out my window, I also started to notice the contrast between front yards and backyards. Front yards had neatly manicured lawns and crisply trimmed bushes, pristine cars, and candy-apple red bicycles. Backyards appeared like graveyards of junk, things people thought were no longer needed, no longer useful. The things out back were unwanted or fragmented or damaged or forgotten. For years, in some cases, these backyard things had been left unexplored and without purpose, out of sight and sometimes covered over—yet still there. For many, grief feels like something to be relegated to "junk" status, exiled to the backyard, where it is inaccessible, unimportant, no longer exerting influence. We don't want these backyard things; we want to forget about them. But as Richard von Weizsäcker, the first president of a reunited Germany, reminds us, "Seeking to forget makes exile all the longer; the secret to redemption lies in remembrance." So too with grief.

THAT 3,300-MILE, 140-HOUR TRAIN JOURNEY became a microcosm of my work, of creating a space where acknowledging grief was not merely welcomed or encouraged but sacrosanct. And now, with this book, I invite you to join me in bearing witness to the myriad faces and shared heart of grief as together we reclaim our fully human wholeness.

Joanne Kyouji Cacciatore
Sedona, Arizona

1

The Role of Others in Our Grief

And we wept that one so lovely should have a life so brief.
—WILLIAM CULLEN BRYANT

I MET KYLE'S MOM through my work with bereaved parents. Her fourteen-year-old son had been struck and killed by a stray bullet. Although it was not intended for him, all fourteen years of him were murdered—by a person who would never be found and would never face prosecution.

"I hate grief! I don't want it anymore! I want you to make it stop! It's killing me!" Karen screamed and cried on my office floor as I sat cross-legged and silent beside her. Her tears were so profuse they fell onto her beige linen pants, staining them with the blue mascara she wore to work every morning in an attempt to cover up her anguish. Karen was a single mom and Kyle her only child—her "entire world." The day he died her life and identity changed, she said. She felt pressure from others to move on and wanted to "feel normal" again.

She recounted a story of how her cousin introduced her to a childless colleague as also being childless. This was a turning point into isolation for Karen. From that moment on, she no longer considered herself a mother. Her sleep had changed, and she stopped attending church. She withdrew from friends and felt unsafe in the world. She moved out of the home where she had raised Kyle into an apartment in a nearby suburb.

Karen came to me six months after Kyle died, wanting help to "overcome" her grief, wanting me to "make her better." There was a familiar desperate edge to our interactions on both our parts. She found herself fantasizing about dying in order to be with Kyle. She didn't literally want to die; she simply wished, with all her might, to rewind time. She wanted Kyle back. His return was the only thing that would remedy her irremediable pain. Her body, mind, heart, and soul were in a state of protest.

WE ARE OFTEN COLLECTIVELY MESMERIZED following violent, highly publicized, or celebrity deaths. This is commonplace, and there is often a public outpouring of embellished emotion and incongruous grief from strangers. Conversely, deaths like Kyle's that occur under more private, albeit still tragic circumstances that are not publicly known elicit only truncated attention.

In Karen's case, gestures of compassion and support were short-lived. Her role as a mother was negated following her son's untimely death, and this caused her to doubt her own heart. She still *felt* like Kyle's mother, but incessant social edicts persuaded her to mistrust not only her place as Kyle's mom, but also her own rightful emotions—her grief. No one remembered with her. No one would speak of Kyle or validate her grief.

In contrast, because of the news-grabbing way Charlotte Helen Bacon was killed by a shooter in Newtown, Connecticut, people were abuzz with chatter, and many expressed grief over her death, even if they never even knew her.

Twenty first-graders and six staff members were murdered in Sandy Hook Elementary School. It was a horror story that was recapitulated in the mass media for months and even years. The unremitting public coverage left some of those who were personally affected by the death of a child or other loved one feeling helplessly exposed and vulnerable.

I met Charlotte's parents in the summer of 2014. Charlotte, a smart, bold, and tenacious girl who could be "a little sneaky" and certainly spirited, was murdered as she holed up in her school bathroom with her classmates. All but one child in the bathroom died that disastrous day. Charlotte's parents, Joel and JoAnn, grappled with the tragic death of their only daughter while at the same time withstanding public scrutiny and consumption of their very private tragedy. In an open letter, an angry, hurt, and frustrated JoAnn wrote,

On December 14, 2012, a man murdered my daughter and stole her future and stole my future. She was herded into her school bathroom with her classmates and gunned down. Completely vulnerable and defenseless. AND I AM ANGRY. In my experience, anger is the emotion that people dislike the most. They do one of three things: Try to change my attitude and have me look on the "bright side" and "count my blessings," or change the subject, or stop showing up altogether. All of these infuriate me even more. It is a vicious cycle. I can speak my truth and make everyone uncomfortable and have them running for the hills or I can be the great pretender, smiling and nodding my head, making myself feel like a fraud. Both are awful and both leave me feeling isolated and misunderstood.

What I want to know is how anyone can think that I will ever be okay with my daughter's murder? I am outraged, and want to scream, *"Why are you not outraged?"* And as for blessings, you don't want to travel down that road with me. You can count your blessings, but I don't feel very blessed at the moment. You also don't want to remind me that great things come from great tragedy. I do not want to hear how my daughter's death taught you something profound or compelled you to do something. My daughter was not placed on this earth to die and give new perspective. Charlotte was here because she was wanted, was loved, and had something to offer this world while she was living. Everything else feels like an appeasement, and it hurts. What nongrievers like is to find inspiration, the silver lining, and the triumphant end. I despise being told that I am an inspiration. It truly makes me uncomfortable. . . . I am a grieving mother.

JoAnn expresses important points about the ways others perceive grief. These perceptions stir up many emotions within us that can complicate our experience of mourning. For JoAnn, the assumption, explicit or not, that somehow Charlotte's death was meant to inspire others or create a better world is unhelpful. What they have "done with grief"—any legacy since her death—came at far too high a cost for her family. And failing to recognize the deep, unmitigated pain that preceded their "new" and unwanted lives is not honoring.

Cultural norms promote inexplicable double standards that are often harmful to those grieving. Certain tragedies deemed worthy are validated, and in those cases, others often arrogate those losses, usurping a grief that is not theirs. Individual grief is discouraged, even scorned, beyond a brief period of time. Years later, the culture willingly remembers private tragedy publicly without assent, consultation, consideration of those who are personally affected. But if a loss isn't dramatic enough, if it hasn't touched the masses or been deemed worthy of a public platform, then society might not remember at all.

When others call into question our grief, defy our perennial relationship with those we love who have died, treat us as anathema and avoid us, and push us toward healing before we are ready, they simply redouble our burden.

It almost seems that the only way to eradicate our grief would be to relinquish the love we feel—to disassemble our loved one's place in our lives. But checking in with the wisdom of our heart, we see that is impossible.

Grief and love occur in tandem.

2

Public and Private Grief

May there be such a oneness between us that
when one weeps the other tastes salt.
—KAHLIL GIBRAN

ON DECEMBER 22, 2009, Katie and Zack said goodbye to their mom to
meet with friends in their small, southern Arizona town. It was the last
time she saw them. During a sudden dust storm, nine tractor-trailer
rigs and thirteen passenger vehicles collided, creating a firestorm so
intense the street was still steaming eight hours later. That dreadful
crash claimed Katie and Zack's lives. Sandie and Mark, their parents,
suffered an irredeemable loss, one that changed them forever. They
came to see me in Phoenix, a four-hour commute, every other week
for months. Sandie often sat and just wept. Mark did too, though he
favored sharing more freely.

Articulating their grief made Sandie and Mark feel a little better.
Sandie said, "It's like overeating and purging some of it. . . . It allows
a little more room for the sadness that I've been eating so long."

Katie and Zack's deaths were highly publicized, their names
released on TV even before their older brother had been notified.
The media stalked Sandie and Mark for interviews. Startling images
of the crash radiated from television sets around the world. The disre-
spectful ways in which Katie and Zack's deaths were handled by the
mass media, exposing them to insensitive sensationalism, increased
their parents' angst, fear, and isolation. Six years later, the kids' rooms
remain untouched, consecrated space with all things in their intended
places. Friends felt the decision to leave the rooms like that was bad

for Sandie and Mark. Tearful over this reaction, Sandie said that if she changed their rooms, she felt she would lose even more of what little remained of them. Keeping their rooms intact was a symbolic way to stay close to her children—something so many failed to understand. And then, not understanding, these others doubted and judged as if this immense weight were somehow theirs to carry.

As the years passed, a few people offered active compassion, sincerely heartening Sandie and Mark. One teacher at their children's school initiated a memorial walk dedicated to Katie and Zack to fund a scholarship in their memory. Because of Katie's abiding commitment to vegetarianism, Sandie followed in her footsteps and became an herbivore. And because of her children's deep love for animals, she and Mark now rescue dogs.

It has been a long and arduous path for them to arrive at this point.

I REMEMBER THE DAY PRINCESS DIANA'S FUNERAL was televised and millions watched the procession.

That same week, a woman called me, concerned that her sister, whose baby had died during childbirth, wanted to videotape her baby's funeral. The caller felt it was macabre, abnormal, and wanted me to convince her sister not to do it.

"Did you happen to watch Diana's funeral?" I inquired, a little warily. In an instant, she understood. It made no sense to watch a stranger's funeral while questioning her sister's more personal memorial. Princess Di's funeral and the birthday celebrations for Elvis in Graceland are examples of a public invocation of a false interpersonal connection to a stranger. Our culture accepts Graceland as a museum but criticizes Sandie and Mark's rightful decision to leave their children's rooms as they were. Legitimate grief is challenged, while the mourning of stranger-celebrities is glorified. Looked at closely, this really is quite bizarre.

Choices we make as grievers merit the deference of others.

Grievers need to be asked respectfully by their own communities whether and how they would allow their tragedies to be put on public display. We should be able to express our own sorrow and remember our loved ones however we choose. If we are fortunate, communities grace us with generosity without expectation, privacy without isolation, casseroles without gratitude, and the well-intended standard, "I'm here for you," without needing any response from us.

Such community grace, in the comparatively rare times it's present, is so often short-lived, but grief persists. People resettle into the chaos of life swiftly. Normalcy resumes, at least for those who aren't grieving.

But when we are frightened and in pain, we need others with whom we can be honest. We need others who can enter the abyss with us, sometimes again and again. We need to reach out to someone who is safe, who will not judge, who will not shut down or shun our pain. And, when we are hurting this much, we may need to borrow, muster, or scrape up the courage to *reach out* to others. And we need these things for an indefinite period.

Solace and care come from many sources. Others who listen deeply, attentively, and nonjudgmentally can be found in the least expected places. Take note, pay attention, and seek help from those willing to be present with you.

Time with these kinds of people can carry you through perilous terrain.

3

Ritual and Artistic Expressions of Grief

> To love means to open ourselves to grief, sorrow,
> and disappointment as well as to joy, fulfillment,
> and thus an intensity of consciousness that before
> we did not know was possible.
> —ROLLO MAY

DEPENDING ON REGION, RELIGION, AND ETHNICITY, we humans may differ in the ways we ritualize grief, understand grief, and behave as we work our way through it, but grief is the single most unifying aspect of the human experience. Every culture and every religion knows about grief.

Siddhartha Gautama, who would become the Buddha, was bereaved as a child, having lost his mother Mayadevi during infancy. With the crucifixion of Jesus, the Virgin Mary became a bereaved mother. Jesus grieved when his friend Lazarus died, despite his faith in eternal life. Muhammad lost his young son Ibrahim, and he also lost his grandchild. Abraham buried his wife Sarah, and their bereaved son Isaac, according to Torah, took three years to finally find comfort and love again in the arms of his wife Rebekah. In the Baha'i tradition, Bahá'u'lláh's father died in his early youth.

Throughout history, across cultures and religions, grief touches us all. Grief with no fixed expiration date is an inescapable truth of the human condition. Grief, by its very nature, is labyrinthine and enigmatic; its implications are emotional, physical, social and interpersonal, economic, spiritual, and existential.

So many factors affect any specific manifestation of grief: our relationship to the person who died, the way they died, the degree of our love and shared connection, relational dependence, early death rituals, how we're treated during the loss, how we were notified, how others interacted with us in the aftermath, our view of the world, our spiritual path and inclinations, previous history of loss and trauma, and who we are at our core. All these things deeply influence our experience of grief, and grief rituals may be similarly unique.

It is a challenge to teach students about grief when they've never experienced it, but it's not impossible. As a professor at Arizona State University, while my primary focus is research, I teach four courses a year. The most popular course is the one I teach on traumatic death and grief. Students file in for a semester of experiential pedagogy, seeming to understand that as counselors, therapists, administrators, or simply human beings who love, grief will at some point touch their lives. As part of the coursework, I ask students to demonstrate their understanding of grief culminating in a creative arts project.

One excellent example came from a reserved and sensitive student named Theresa:

RECIPE FOR RAW GRIEF

From the Kitchen of Theresa's Heart
Serves: One

INGREDIENTS:
1 heaping cup disbelief
1 tablespoon reluctance to say goodbye
16 ounces excruciating pain
3 cups brutal sadness
2 tablespoons confusion (substitute questioning)
½ cup constant obsessing
8 ounces anger (substitute feeling misunderstood)
2 teaspoons agonizing guilt
¾ cup embarrassment

1 quart loneliness

Dash of untimely and needless

DIRECTIONS: Preheat oven to 1123°. In small bowl, mix disbelief with reluctance to say goodbye. Next, trim platitudes from excruciating pain and discard. Use mixture to coat pain. Cook in scalding cast-iron skillet until blackened. Set aside. Fill large pot with tears and bring to a boil. Lower heat; pour brutal sadness into pot and cover. Allow to simmer for weeks. When sadness is numb, remove from heat and drain tears from pot. Stir confusion and constant obsessing into sadness and set aside. Use mallet to pound anger until tender. Cut into bite size pieces. Fry in pan over high heat with agonizing guilt and embarrassment. When anger turns red, remove pan from heat. To assemble, spread pain into bottom of baking dish. Layer on the sadness mixture, then cover with anger, guilt, and shame. Top with loneliness. Season with untimely and needless. Place in oven and bake until loneliness turns to intense longing. Let sit for a lifetime.

NOTES: *Pairs well with absolute fear. Best served smothered in love and compassion (may need assistance). Garnish with a sense of peace.*

Many students seemed to touch on something similarly important.

One young woman wrote a letter to her sister who had died before she was even born, nearly three decades earlier. She told her sister how she now realized, through this course, what her parents felt in having endured her death. She apologized to her sister for not acknowledging her on holidays and when others asked if she had a sister. She even apologized to her sister for referring to their mother in the letter as "my mother." She promised from that point forward she would recognize her place as the firstborn child in the family. She closed the letter with something like, "I will talk to *our* mother about you and I will remember you."

Another student sculpted a piece of art for her father, who had died by suicide when she was eight. It was a sculpture of him at his last moment, just before his death, with angel's wings wrapped around him. She was, as a little girl, standing before him in the sculpture with her hand outstretched. His eyes were looking at her. She titled the piece *Catharsis*.

Grief education is quintessential to shifting our culture's antagonistic relationship to grief, and expressive, creative arts are an important part of this.

4

Early Manifestations of Grief

Until my ghastly tale is told, this heart within me burns.

—SAMUEL TAYLOR COLERIDGE

ONE MOTHER DESCRIBED THIS SCENE, in which she learned of her son's death:

> The doctor came into the room. It was after midnight. He said, as cold and detached and unemotional as anything I've ever heard: "There was nothing we could do. He's dead." And then he left the room and we were all alone again except for the hospital chaplain who looked terrified. . . . I didn't even cry. I didn't really understand. I mean, I heard the words but . . . I left my body. I didn't get back into my body for months. I still can't believe he's gone.

Initially, we may hear such news with our ears alone—and not yet with our hearts. The depth and breadth of the loss is unfathomable, and its full impact is never realized immediately, but only gradually over time. The mind tries to protect us from near-lethal initial shock, and a type of emotional anesthesia often ensues so that we may feel as if we are in a movie or operating in slow motion. Sounds, figures, and movements change, and we may exist in a profoundly altered state of consciousness.

Slowly, as the shock of loss gradually withdraws its numbing veil, an indescribable pain arises from the innermost pit of our bellies. This pain brings with it feelings we may never have felt—unfamiliar and hideously distressing. Everything in us wants to run from the reality of loss, yet the agony demands to be felt. It calls and recalls our attention repeatedly to the details. In a sense, the process of mourning is an outward expression of that love that now has no physical or interpersonal place to be enacted.

It's not unusual for bereaved parents, children, siblings, grandparents, and spouses to experience damage to their sense of self, persistent yearning for the one who died, and a desire to escape the pain by any means—including death of the self. Many parents with whom I've worked tell me they feel their old self, the person they had been, has died. Some people report feelings of guilt and shame at their loved one's death—even when, from the outside, these emotions seem unjustified. Bereaved parents, for example, expect their children will outlive them, and to bury a child feels unnatural, out of order, and incites a paralyzing, heart-shattering grief. These feelings are common and normal, albeit painful, for those grieving a significant loss. Deep despair, agitation and impatience, apathy, anhedonia, and a lack of interest in things that once mattered are also frequently reported—and also quite normal.

What parent whose child has died would not experience a yearning to reestablish that potent bond? What child would not feel unsafe, afraid, and abandoned in the world when his or her parent dies? What person would not experience a sometimes crushing loneliness upon the death of a partner? Amid such loss, all of life's meaning can be called into question.

Fear, excessive worry, and anxiety often appear. When our beloved dies, we become acutely aware of death, our own and others' finitude—in a phenomenon termed *mortality salience*—and we begin to grapple with this reality. Along with this, a person may experience heightened states of sensory awareness and environmental sensitivity that may abet fear-based distress, especially for other loved ones. We become aware and afraid that they, too, may die. Envy toward others who still have what we have lost often arises, and anger—even rage—may also come up.

Grief reveals itself in both subtle and dramatic behaviors—particularly when we are not willing to feel what grief requires of us. Substance abuse, gambling, overconsumerism, promiscuity, interpersonal conflict, recklessness, and even suicidal gestures are common manifestations of this dynamic. We may find it more difficult—if not impossible—to concentrate for very long on anything but the loss. Obviously, this can make it difficult to work, though not necessarily impossible when surrounded by supportive colleagues. Conversely, some may immerse themselves in work or exercise or spirituality explicitly seeking to avoid thinking of the loss and the feelings associated with it.

Responses to grief can take the form of absence—of pleasure, of concentration, and so on—and they can also take the form of presence. I've worked with some bereaved individuals who report extraordinary sensory experiences: they may see, hear, or smell things that others do not. Some report "signs" from their loved ones, often in the form of symbols like butterflies or meaningfully related numbers. A significant minority report sleep-related hallucinations, either dreaming or on the edge of sleep; some are frightful and others comforting.

Interpersonal relationships may become strained, and in grieving families, this may be amplified. As grievers, we may feel tired and may not have the energy to engage with others in meaningful ways. We may feel less patient and tolerant. Perhaps we have not yet learned how to openly share our feelings, or we have not found others willing to deeply listen, or we do not feel safe doing so. Many grievers report that they lose old friends—and sometimes gain new ones—as their dyadic relationships shift.

Children in family systems may feel overlooked—or what I call "invisibilized"—and parents may lose track of the fact that their children are grieving too. In a grieving family, suffering happens at the individual and collective levels. Every person is grieving and acting out that grief in his or her own way, and each person is enacting that grief in relationship to others. In such circumstances, both the spaces within us and the spaces between us become heavy-laden with grief.

The almost physical weight of grief can directly affect the body, leading to changes in appetite, weight, energy levels, and sleep patterns as well as other problems. Some report trouble breathing and sensory malfunctions such as a loss in the ability to taste or smell. Others complain of diffuse pain, aching arms, chest pain, back pain, headaches, and lethargy that manifest for the first time after the loss. All of these may be a result of the sustained—but normal—psychological stress associated with grief. Even so, grief can be associated with premature mortality of the griever, especially a bereaved parent—though studies show this may be related to the effects of chronic stress and waning self-care rather than a medical crisis.

The emotional, spiritual, existential, and physical states that accompany grief leave grievers feeling quite vulnerable in an environment sometimes hostile to grief and the mortality salience it brings with it. Many families with whom I've worked say their fragility in early grief made them want to withdraw from their perceivedly unresponsive surroundings post-loss. Many grievers feel implicit or explicit social pressure to "feel better" or "move on," and the incongruence between the messages of how they should feel and the inner wisdom of what they actually *do* feel causes many to doubt their own hearts. This lack of alignment between self and the other is one more way in which *avoidable* and *irrational* suffering is imposed on grievers in the middle of *natural*—which is to say unavoidable and rational—suffering.

The ways we treat our grief and the way others approach us in it truly matter—as does our grief itself. The Spanish philosopher Miguel de Unamuno said that "man dies of cold, not of darkness." When I was in the early throes of grieving Cheyenne, that darkness (and it was for me pure blackness at times) was excruciating beyond words—but did not threaten to kill me. Much more dangerous in my already fragile state was the coldness of others—the chronic loneliness, the fight for my dead child's dignity, the dismissive comments, and the way so many people around me turned away from the ugly, terrifying face of grief. These are the things that unhinged me.

Darkness does not kill—but cold can.

On the other hand, grief also has the potential to bring us closer to the warmth, love, and connection that is within us and between us. When others meet us with nonjudging compassion, we experience a sense of belonging that polishes the rough edges of grief. But when we are pushed by our culture, this cult of pleasure, to heal on a fixed timescale or to somehow "choose happiness" over grief, when we are socially constrained and unable to give expression to our emotions, we feel unsafe, misunderstood, and isolated. And when this happens we may, to the detriment of humanity, retract from the world as we begin to, quite rightly, feel frightened and mistrusting of the way our honest grief will be met.

At such times, grievers are often blamed for failing to "grow" or "move on" or "find meaning," and this blame is both unfair and utterly misplaced. To help those grieving, society needs to provide us all a place to rest our minds and hearts: a place fertile with loving kindness and compassion—not judgment, coercion, and scrutiny.

Only there, only when ready, will we be able to blossom (albeit painfully) into a joy that cohabitates with grief—rather than displacing or replacing it.

LET US RETURN to the example of Karen and the death of her fourteen-year-old son Kyle. Others chided Karen not to talk about Kyle's death because it makes her feel so sad. Such injurious advice often comes from others' unwillingness to bear witness to pain because witnessing pain causes them to feel their own pain and dread.

After encountering this attitude in others, Karen found it had become much more difficult to process and integrate the grief she was so rightfully feeling. Karen's traumatic grief then became more psychologically destructive to her than in its original state. In a fundamental way, Kyle's death shattered the façade of her former existence, ravaged her identity, and simultaneously brought her face-to-face with what it means to be human: to feel vulnerable, to suffer, to fear, and to risk grief for the sake of love. The superfluous burden of *avoidance* inflicted by others heightened her self-doubt, loneliness, fear, and repression of herself—in a way that became painfully unhinging for her.

Eventually, though, with support that honored and made space for her grief rather than colluding to avoid it, Karen came to understand that the kind of love she'd shared with Kyle for fourteen years is not something that was to be "gotten over," dismissed, or treated as if it didn't matter. At the center of it, this is the love of a mother for her child, an incomparable and nonpareil relationship that doesn't end with a child's death. What Karen told me she wanted, initially, was to "overcome" her grief, but through our work together, what she later realized she wanted was to feel all that called out to be felt, in short to have the "courage to suffer."

Suffer is an interesting word that can usefully be defined as "having the capacity to endure pain without having to change it, resist it, or cling to it." My work with Karen started with providing a space in which she could feel safe being with her feelings without any pressure or expectations. It was space in which to remember Kyle and to express her love. Through this, Karen came to trust herself again.

She learned that grief was not the enemy and that its shadow would not swallow or annihilate her. She adapted, made space for the grief to exist, and allowed it to be whatever it was, moment by moment. Eventually, she started to notice that she was able to endure, to suffer, and the edges of grief softened on their own and in their own time. Karen had felt disconnected from her body, and so she and I also worked on the physicality of trauma. We hiked together, sometimes barefoot. Eventually, when she felt ready, she took up yoga. She began to reinhabit both her mind and her body.

Today, Karen knows that place in her heart—that venerated and venerable place—where Kyle's name is inscribed. She can visit it when necessary—even if it "levels" her for a while. She knows that the storm below the thunderclouds is only part of the story, and the sun still shines above them. She trusts that any darkened tunnel in which she finds herself will eventually end and release her into the light of the world, again and again. And, though long stretches of time pass when grief doesn't come into her foreground, she knows it is always there, quiet, in the background.

When grief asks to be seen, she meets it and embraces it as she would a visit from an old friend.

And now, she tells me, she wouldn't want it any other way.

5

Nutrient-Deficient Soil

There is, I am convinced, no picture that conveys in all its
dreadfulness, a vision of sorrow, despairing, remediless,
supreme. If I could paint such a picture, the canvas would
show only a woman looking down at her empty arms.

—CHARLOTTE BRONTË

I SPENT MUCH OF THE FIRST FEW YEARS after Cheyenne died defending
the dignity of my grief. And I would often collapse under the weight
of the pressure to "heal"—which seemed to me like being pressured
to forget.

I remember a phone call from a dear friend in November of 1994
to wish me a "happy birthday." It had only been four months since
Chey's death, and I was most certainly not my usual self. "What's
wrong?" she said—perhaps hearing quiet despair in my voice. "I don't
want to celebrate. I can't celebrate. She's dead." My friend proceeded
to lecture me on how I should be grateful for my other children and
how I should be celebrating and having fun: "You're wallowing in
your grief, and its time to get it together and leave that behind you."

The conversation ended with me in tears—then I sat down and
wrote this in my journal, imagining it to be a letter to my friend:

This is my path. It was not a path of my choice, but it is a path
I must walk mindfully and with intention. It is a journey through
grief that takes time. Every cell in my body aches. I may be impatient, distracted, frustrated, and unfocused. I won't want to
celebrate anything. I may get angry more easily, or I may seem

hopeless. I will shed many, many, many tears. I won't smile as often as my old self. Smiling hurts now. Most everything hurts some days, even breathing.

But please, just sit beside me.

Say nothing.

Do not offer a cure.

Or a pill, or a word, or a potion.

Witness my suffering and don't turn away from me.

Please be gentle with me.

Please, self, be gentle with me, too.

I will not ever "get over it" so please don't urge me down that path. Even if it seems like I am having a good day, maybe I am even able to smile for a moment, the pain is just beneath the surface of my skin. My chest has a nearly constant sinking pain and sometimes I feel as if I will explode from the grief.

Don't tell me how I should or shouldn't be doing it or that I should or shouldn't "feel better by now." Don't tell me that "God has a plan" for me. Don't tell me what's right or wrong. I'm doing it my way, in my time.

I have a new normal now. Oh, perhaps as time passes, I will discover new meanings and insights about what her death means to me. Perhaps, one day, when I am very old, I will say that time has truly helped to heal my broken heart. But always remember that not a second of any minute of any hour of any day passes when I am not aware of the presence of her absence, no matter how many years lurk over my shoulder.

Please, be kind to me.

I never sent this letter to her.

I was too frightened and wounded, so instead, I stopped answering her calls. This single contact with her widened the gorge between others and me. It would take a few more years and the ignition of some fire in my belly before I would learn how to use my voice when others battered me with their words.

Others may tell us that it's time to "move on" or that this is "part of some bigger plan"—because our shattering makes them feel uneasy, vulnerable, at risk. Some may avoid us, others pity us. But this grief is ours.

We have earned this grief, paying for it with love and steadfast devotion. We own this pain, even on days when we wish it weren't so. We needn't give it away or allow anything, or anyone, to pilfer it.

Through the grief and the love we can hold our heads high—even in tears, even shattered.

What's ours is ours—and *rightfully*.

6

Cultural Sensitivity

The ordinary response to atrocities is to banish them
from consciousness. Certain violations . . . are too terrible
to utter aloud: this is the meaning of the word *unspeakable*.
Atrocities, however, refuse to be buried.

—JUDITH HERMAN

I RECEIVED A CALL early one Saturday morning. It was the chief medical examiner for the office at which I volunteered as family liaison. "Hurry down, please," she said. She went on to explain that a baby had just died, and his body had been transported for an autopsy to determine a cause of death, but the family refused to consent. "They're from the reservation," she said. "This is a real problem for us."

It seemed clear enough to me: "So then don't do the autopsy." But she reminded me, according to state law, an autopsy *must* be performed on all sudden deaths. There exists only one exception in the state: if the death occurs on a sovereign nation—a reservation—of one of the Native American peoples. While this child had lived on the sovereign nation, he was transported by helicopter to a local hospital, which is where he actually died.

There were two middle-aged couples and a young couple standing in close proximity in the parking lot awaiting my arrival. One of the elder men, Henry, whom I later identified as the paternal grandfather, stepped forward, setting himself apart from the group. I introduced myself to him only—not approaching or making eye contact with any other family member. Once inside the office, I offered some water, tissues, and my assurance that I would act as their advocate. I

felt no emotion from the family, not even grief. But the younger couple sat in the corner chairs and held each other, their heads bowed as
if in prayer. Henry alone was looking at me, so I spoke directly, and
only, to him.

"I'm just so very sorry," I said. "Would you tell me the story?"

Henry explained that his grandson, Joseph, had been a healthy,
thriving eighteen-month-old. Joseph became ill very suddenly, and
after the onset of a fever, his parents—the young couple in the corner—
consulted with the medicine man. Joseph's symptoms persisted the
rest of the day so Henry urged them to go to their medical center.
Shortly after their arrival at the medical center, Joseph had a seizure
and he was airlifted to the local hospital, where he was pronounced
dead a few hours later. The attending physicians sent Joseph's body
for autopsy and informed the family—who then began to protest the
procedure: autopsies are forbidden in their sovereign nation.

As Henry told the story, I noticed other family members began
to cry, huddling in the corner, holding on to one another. Joseph's
mother and father were shaking. "We don't permit autopsies where
we come from!" Henry said. "It interferes with the ascension of the
spirit. It is a violation of our customs." Again, I assured him that I
would advocate for his family. I took a few minutes to explain the
usual protocol at the medical examiner's office.

With his consent, I went into the back office. Only one medical
examiner worked on Saturday. I talked to her about the family and
reinforced the need to respect their culture and customs. Understanding this, she offered an alternative. "If we can start with x-rays and
laboratory tests, we may be able to find the cause of death without
having to autopsy," she said. "Will they allow this?"

Back in the waiting room, Henry agreed to this option.

Together in silence, for two hours, we awaited the results. Henry
led his family in native prayers, spoken softly under their breath. I
kept company with them the entire time but sitting on the other side
of the room and remaining silent.

Eventually, the medical examiner asked to see me through the security window partitioning the waiting area from the back offices, and this was the first time that the family members made eye contact with me. Henry looked at me and I looked back. "I'll be right back," I said.

The medical examiner had indeed found the cause of death without needing to perform an autopsy: Joseph had developed an intestinal obstruction that became infected. He died of sepsis. Both the medical examiner and I went into the waiting room to inform the family. I spoke directly to Henry, and as the medical examiner listened, Henry's head dropped. The family began to cry as I explained the cause of Joseph's death. Henry remained emotionless. I said, "I'm just so sorry, Henry. Do you have any questions that I can answer for you?"

"No," he said softly.

"Henry, would you like to see Joseph?" I asked. From the corner of my eye, I saw Joseph's young mother look up, wide-eyed, but she said nothing.

Henry responded, "No, no, no. We don't want to see him. We must not." There was complete silence in the room. Concerned that I may have offended Henry, I quickly apologized, explaining that I was unfamiliar with their beliefs. I wanted to give them some time alone as a family, so I asked permission to leave.

When I returned to the waiting room, Henry's wife immediately approached me. "We want to see Joseph. We have decided to see him," she said. Henry nodded in affirmation. I went into the back office immediately and prepared a small office for them to use. I made a bed out of an office desk, putting layers of blankets and pillows on it to make a kind of cradle for the dead boy, for Joseph. I brought in enough chairs for everyone and dimmed the lights.

I returned with Joseph a few minutes later, wrapped in a warmed blanket. Henry quickly stood up and looked directly at me. He paused a moment, looked down at Joseph, and then gently he took him from my arms. His face softened. Everyone was still. Henry held Joseph in his arms and began to talk to him in their native language. He kissed Joseph's feet, his arms, and his cheeks. He wept. Everyone wept. Henry tied a sacred healing feather, used earlier that day by their medicine man, to Joseph's shirt, and then Henry passed the child to his wife. Over more than two hours, each family member took a turn to say goodbye.

At one point, I thought I should leave—telling Henry I wanted to give them privacy. He grabbed my arm and asked, "Please—stay with us. You're one of us now." Eventually they said their final good-byes and, reluctantly, placed Joseph back into my arms.

The family waited for me in the parking lot.

I told them that I would be available if they had any questions or needed anything in the future. I thanked them for their patience and said my final goodbye, walking back to the office. Then Joseph's young mother yelled out across the parking lot. I stopped at the door and turned. She walked toward me, slowly, and then began to run. The others followed. She wrapped her arms around me and began to cry.

"Thank you so much," she said over and over. Her young husband came up behind her, embracing us both and began to cry, also thanking me. Then, one by one, the grandparents surrounded me in an embrace.

I'd learned so much from them. I'd learned how to be a student, a beginner, how to set aside my own beliefs to help others. I'd learned about patience and the power of silence.

And I bowed in gratitude to Joseph, my teacher.

JOSEPH'S DEATH, like so many of the others in this book, was trau-matic for those who loved him. Yet compassion and love softened the edges of that trauma for Joseph's family—and for me. The cir-cumstances surrounding deaths that are traumatic in nature may be severely worsened by the way people are notified of death, by unskillful grief-denying therapy, by legalities and insensitive actions—medical, spiritual, and community-based—that do not take into account the context of trauma and its effects. Joseph's death was traumatic for his parents, and nothing I could do would change that. But I could mitigate additional suffering for them as a result of fearful and grief-avoidant people and bureaucracies unprepared to deal with or understand the realities and consequences of traumatic grief.

Traumatic death provokes traumatic grief. And *traumatic death* refers to any sudden and unexpected death, violent or disfiguring death, death following prolonged suffering, suicide, homicide, and the death of a child at any age and from any cause. When someone we love dies traumatically, we feel frighteningly uprooted, markedly insecure, and our ability to trust in the world feels gravely threatened—and indeed it *is* gravely threatened.

The effects of trauma have both a psychological and physiological edge. This can manifest as increased respiration and heart rate, dilated pupils, cognitive and memory impairment, hyperarousal, intrusive thoughts and images, feeling out of body or depersonalized, alterations in time perception, emotional blunting, and experiential avoidance. This last one—trying to avoid or not feel something—is, arguably, one of the most maladaptive responses to traumatic grief.

In an attempt to not feel, a griever may fall into a state of constant distraction-seeking. Drugs and alcohol, television, food, exercise, sex, gambling, shopping, interpersonal conflict, and even spiritual practice can become unconscious pawns in a chess game with avoidance of our pain. Humans are creative with distractions, and the options are myriad. We can use anything to take us away from our feelings. Staying still, just being with world-shattering grief, is simply too threatening without the right kind of support and a feeling of both physical and emotional safety.

The body's reaction to a threat is to run away, to resist the threat, or to become emotionally paralyzed by the threat—this is the *flight, fight, or freeze response*. It occurs when a cascade of complex physiological reactions are set into motion after any type of physical or psychological threat is perceived. In less than half a second, the brain releases neurochemicals that function as a type of biological alarm system in reaction to the danger. In cases when the danger is short-term, action is taken, and the threat passes, we quickly return to a state of equilibrium.

After traumatic grief, however, returning to homeostasis requires more support for much longer than many people realize and allow. Traumatic grief is a sustained state of disequilibrium to which the mourning person *cannot* adjust. This is amplified by the fact that habituation and adaptation to threat cannot occur in a society fearful of suffering and pain, one that pathologizes the authentic expression of emotions and lacks appropriate support structures and rituals to remember and honor the dead. Such a society pushes mourners to assign more negative self-judgments and erroneous meaning to their grief reactions. This may include ascribing to ourselves inadequate adjustment ("I should feel better by now."), personal incompetence ("What is wrong with me?"), or even mental illness ("I have major depression.").

Such erroneous beliefs about grieving lead to suppression, distraction, and avoidance of natural grief reactions—in short, they lead to vastly more suffering.

7

Bearing the Unbearable

Though I think not
to think about it,
I do think about it
and shed tears
thinking about it.
—RYOKAN

CHEYENNE HAD DIED only a few months earlier. I had three young children, and I was trying with all my might to stay present with them. I felt lonely, *so lonely*, inside the grief. And I was terrified.

I weighed barely ninety pounds. Food stuck in my throat.

I couldn't get anyone to *really* listen, despite trying three therapists who "specialized" in grief in rapid succession. The first counselor suggested I go to church. Within fifteen minutes, the second counselor referred me to a psychiatrist for medications. The meeting with the final therapist, Bill, a man of modest stature with thick Buddy Holly–style glasses, lasted the longest before I felt the familiar urge to run from the office screaming. Bill tried to be kind, but he kept forcibly redirecting the conversation from my grief and my suffering to my marital relationship.

I'd brought a few photos of Cheyenne, and he quickly looked—handing them back, like a child playing hot potato, without a hint of reverence. He didn't get it. And I felt worse than I had when I'd come in.

As I left, I looked at him and asked—sincerely and out of abiding sadness—"Do you have children of your own?"

Bill answered, "Yes, and my wife is pregnant with another."

I was dismayed. I could not imagine that a person who had experienced love for a child would not be capable of deeper insight into how such a loss would feel.

"Well, I hope you never have to go through this hell yourself," I said, and I walked out.

Was this all there was for me? If so, I was uncertain I was going to survive.

My mother, hearing that I'd now struck out with three therapists, came over the next morning. My other children, ages three, six, and eight, were playing in the sunroom. I was sitting on the couch staring at the cottonwood tree waving in the wind.

Grief had became my most needy child—grief and the bihourly breast pumping I did to relieve the pain of engorgement. My mother and many others were deeply concerned and said so. The children, meanwhile, gladly ate Snickers for breakfast, a recent morning trend totally uncharacteristic of the health-conscious mother I'd prided myself on being before Chey died. I tried so diligently to stay connected to them, even as I felt the sting of disconnection from my own heart.

I didn't know how to cope in a world that would acknowledge neither my grief nor my love for my daughter. I felt mounting shame for Cheyenne's death and for being unable to care for my three other children.

My mother wanted me to put this behind me, wanted me to be who I was before she died. She was hurting for my pain. When my mother left that morning, I pulled my knees up onto the flowery couch and bowed my head, sobbing aloud. My three-year-old heard the cries from the sunroom and found her way to the arm of the couch. She stroked my hair and said, "Oh Mommy, it's okay to cry and it's okay to be sad because babies aren't supposed to die." I felt tremendous gratitude for the wisdom and compassion of this little child.

LATER THAT NIGHT, I found the energy to pull down a puzzle from the top shelf of the coat closet. It was a 100-piece nature puzzle of the

Havasu Falls in the Grand Canyon. The children were excited, and we each took turns placing our piece into the puzzle. We all agreed: the picture on the puzzle box was of the most magnificently beautiful place we'd seen.

"Mom, let's go there one day," said my eldest.

And we finished the puzzle—except for one last piece. The missing piece belonged in the upper right, near the corner—a small fragment of azure sky.

"I don't have it," he said.

"It must be here somewhere," I told him.

We looked around, under the couch and table, in the closet, standing up and spinning, but we could not find that missing piece. I even offered the kids a reward, one dollar, if they found it. Even so, they quickly lost interest—as children do—and retreated to their sunroom.

And then it hit me.

Of course there was a missing piece.

Looking at the almost-completed puzzle, I could see the vast beauty of the scene—but there was a piece missing. And every time I looked at that puzzle, before I would be able to appreciate the beauty in the picture, I would first see that there, *right there*, is a hole—a missing piece.

And nothing but that one specific, unique piece could ever fit in that spot.

A FEW MONTHS LATER I was still flailing, my grief very much in the foreground, only now what little support I had in the early weeks had all but expired—perishable just like the coleslaw that someone left at my door the second week after she died. One night the phone rang. I answered. A trembling male voice asked for me. "This is she," I said. "This is Bill. Do you remember me? You came to see me after your child died. I'm ashamed to say I don't remember her name." I said timidly, "Yes, I remember you. And her name is Cheyenne." He started to weep—loudly. And I was confused.

He then asked if I would come to his office. I hesitated. "Are you okay?" I asked.

"No," he answered. "We . . . lost our baby . . . I'm so sorry for the way I treated you. I get it now," he said. "I get it now."

I got in my car and drove to him.

8

Pause, Reflect, and Feel Meaning

We have only one reality and that is the here and now.
What we miss by our evasions will never return. . . .
Each day is precious: a moment can be everything.
—KARL JASPERS

HOW DO WE BEAR THAT WHICH IS UNBEARABLE? How do we suffer that which is insufferable? How do we endure that which is unendurable? Early grief feels wild, primitive, nonlinear, and crazed. It commands our assent and our attention; it uses up all the oxygen in the room; it erupts unpredictably. Our minds replay grief-related content in habitual cycles. It feels inescapable and lasts for much longer than other people, the nonbereaved, think it should. Like an open, bleeding wound it begs our tending.

"I am here," grief says. "Be careful with me. Stop. Pause. Stay with me."

I STARTED KARATE IN THE 1980s, and in karate we practice basic sets of movements called *kata*. The movements flow from one to the next—with one crucial but often overlooked aspect: the pause. The pause in the kata is about *holding*, being still, waiting, listening deeply. It is about creating space and allowing the last movement a dignified ending before beginning the next movement.

That pause is an art—and as such it is much like grieving. The pause is what happens between words, between breaths, and between moments of what is and what isn't. We remember to hold and take a few deep, slow, long breaths.

The word *selah* (Hebrew: הֶלָס)—"to pause, reflect, and feel meaning"—appears almost seventy times in the poetry of the Psalms. Grief by its nature is poetical, elegiac. And poetry, like grief, is subversive, unbridled, and disobedient. Poetry violates linguistic norms because it must. Poetry helps us feel. And when we allow ourselves to feel that which is legitimately ours to feel, we rebel against the rigid grief-denying structures of society.

JIM IS A FIFTY-YEAR-OLD FATHER who lost his eldest son, Mark, to suicide at age twenty-three, nearly three years before seeking counseling. He'd attended several support groups in the immediate weeks following his son's death but then stopped going because he felt "awkward." Jim described himself as dysfunctional, noting that he went to his job every day but had withdrawn from friends and social activities because of what he perceived to be the insensitivity of others toward his loss. This is an important point: he frequently reported feeling alone and abandoned by others, even those who knew and loved his son.

Jim had lost considerable weight over the past few years, and suffered from insomnia, nightmares, intense emotional outbursts, paralyzing anger, and intrusive thoughts of his son's death. Over time, Jim started to avoid thinking about his son and even removed photographs of him from the walls of his home. He sought counseling when he realized the quality of his relationship with his surviving child was suffering. During our first visit lasting two and a half hours, there were many moments of prolonged, emotion-laden silence. In that first session, Jim felt, for the first time, his grief had been "heard and seen."

Our early sessions focused on being with grief unconditionally and nonjudgmentally, and I told Jim I was willing to join him even in what he called "the dark places." This meant he could be honest about his emotions, trusting that I would accept and meet anything he presented. Soon he began setting aside time for daily contemplative meditation—special periods when he would practice just being with his feelings starting with ten minutes in both the morning and evening. He began to keep an emotion journal.

During our fifth session, Jim focused on an amorphous rage he felt. We discussed what mindful rage might look like and how he might go about mindfully feeling it in response to people or situations. We came up with the following six steps for doing this:

1. Recognizing anger/rage as it arose within him while it was happening.
2. Approaching the anger with curiosity and openness.
3. Asking: What is this anger in this moment really about for me?
4. Taking some deep, slow breaths.
5. As needed, walking away from the situation/person.
6. Using progressive muscle relaxation during times when he felt like "blowing up."

By the tenth session, Jim felt substantial relief from his rage, confirmed by his emotion journal, which we reviewed weekly. His sleep patterns began to improve and nightmares ceased. By the thirteenth session, he'd regained eight pounds.

When Jim felt he was ready, we began to more actively approach his grief. This included becoming increasingly aware of nuanced and sometimes conflicted feelings around his son's death. Jim recognized a previously undiscovered sense of guilt and shame tied to his son's suicide. He realized he believed that others must perceive his son as "weak" and think Jim hadn't done enough to help him. This unearthed a strong sense of parental responsibility, culminating in a very emotional disclosure: Jim felt his son's death was ultimately his fault.

I encouraged Jim to write a series of letters to Mark wherein Jim expressed his feelings of failure as a parent. He wrote about the times he wasn't there for Mark and wrote about all the events he'd missed during Mark's childhood. He expressed his regret for not having answered Mark's call on the day of his suicide. And then, in those letters, I encouraged Jim to ask for Mark's forgiveness.

I asked Jim to wait at least thirty minutes and then, in the same journal, write a reply from Mark: "What would Mark say to you, now that you've asked his forgiveness?"

This was a powerful exercise for Jim. He said he "cried until he had no tears left," and that "it felt so good." He said to me, "I could almost hear his voice, saying, *Dad, I love you.*"

As Jim dealt with some of the guilt and shame, his relationship with his surviving son improved, and he began making new friends. He also began attending a support group for bereaved parents every month—and kept going. He eventually regained all the weight he had lost and was able to talk about Mark freely, even putting his photos of Mark back up around the house.

About two years after Jim and I met, he expressed a desire to help other bereaved fathers. He is now a regular volunteer who has assisted many other grieving parents since.

Jim learned to *be with* his grief, to surrender to it—and then found he could do something with it.

9

The Terror beneath the Terror

Love anything, and your heart will certainly be wrung
and possibly be broken. . . . The only place outside
Heaven where you can be perfectly safe from all the
dangers and perturbations of love is Hell.

—C.S. LEWIS

American novelist and bereaved father Mark Twain once said that the "fear of death follows the fear of life." Fear, even terror, might play an important role as it relates to the way we approach—or avoid—our own grief. It also influences the way that others approach (or avoid) our grief.

Scholar Sheldon Solomon proposed a theory that I think explains the reasons grief (and by extension grievers) and death (and by extension those dying or in proximity to death) are treated with such lack of care and even disdain within our social structures. Solomon built his theory, called terror management theory, on the work of cultural anthropologist Ernest Becker, author of the Pulitzer Prize–winning book, *The Denial of Death*.

Becker's work proposes that human beings, at some point in their consciousness, become aware of their own mortality, and then because of the death anxiety such awareness evokes, people must suppress the subsequent anxious emotions and thoughts in order to function in an otherwise terrifying world where everyone and everything will die.

Culture's main function, according to Becker, is to help us suppress those thoughts and feelings and to maintain order. This helps us feel immortal, invulnerable, and strong. Denial of death is, in a sense, a refutation of the authentic, mortal self—and it is pervasive because it helps us to manage our sense of terror.

A theory of mortality salience proposes that if a person reports high death anxiety and fear, he or she is more likely to go into a type of denial and avoidance. This is because, consciously or unconsciously, the person perceives a threat. Thus, the individual who is scared of death (or grief) will construct other defenses to temporarily relieve any distress. Those defenses serve as an unconscious *false exemption* constructed in the mind against the prospect of inevitable suffering: "That dead person cannot be me. I cannot lose my loved ones. I cannot be that vulnerable."

I have witnessed this individual avoidance as a microcosm of what occurs in communities. The same terror is present in avoidance-colluding larger systems: churches, schools, communities, and, broadly speaking, cultural groups. Despite the fact that we will all experience the death of someone we love, something in the social system pushes back against that reality, creating a type of systemic avoidance that promotes hostility, intolerance, and segregation of those grieving.

I once received a call from a concerned grade-school counselor. A nine-year-old girl whose mother had died only weeks earlier was asked to leave the room by her teacher as the other students were making Mother's Day cards. Rather than talk to this bereaved child about her mother's death and ask her if she, too, would like to make a card, perhaps to take to the cemetery, the teacher literally isolated her in another room. Lacking any training in death awareness and grief education, the teacher was frightened to stir up emotions in the girl—and, one presumes, in herself and others as well. The counselor and I worked on remedying this by allowing the child to make a card, which she intently wanted to do, and providing some psychoeducational materials on the appropriate support for grieving children to her teacher and other school administrators.

In a death- and grief-avoidant culture, a grieving person becomes the other to whom social structures cannot, and will not, relate—and that avoidance is truly tragic.

Contemplating the death of those we love and feeling tremendous grief in the aftermath of so doing brings us face-to-face with what matters. It shows us what it means to be human is to be vulnerable, to suffer, and to risk love.

10

The Pursuit of Happiness and the Unity of Opposites

The road up and the road down
is one and the same.

—HERACLITUS

FOR ALL WHO LOVE, SUFFERING IS INEVITABLE.

To love deeply is one of life's most profound gifts, and the loss of a loved one is one of life's most profound tragedies. That they can happen simultaneously and that we somehow manage to, one day, find even a morsel of joy in our hearts again are profoundly and wonderfully mysterious.

Yet our grief-phobic culture numbs us to this. "Just think happy thoughts!" it says, "You can *choose* to be happy!"

The "pursuit of happiness" is enshrined in no lesser place than the U.S. Constitution. But what if we have this all wrong?

Viktor Frankl, Holocaust survivor and author of the seminal book *Man's Search for Meaning*, cautioned us about pursuing happiness. He said that we cannot chase happiness and expect that we will attain it. Happiness can only arise as a *byproduct* of a life devoted to the service of others—a view that undermines the very foundation upon which the happiness-peddlers have built their platform.

There is an enormous hidden cost for us, as humans, to this relentless obsession with happiness: we lose our willingness and ability to be vulnerable, and we forfeit our connection to self, other, and the natural world—and most especially to our honest, authentic, legitimate grief.

The mischaracterization of grief as abnormal is pervasive. Some mental health providers claim to possess a special treatment for grief. Some physicians and psychiatrists will prescribe medications to tame grief. Some life coaches claim they can "cure" grief in less than three sessions. Even some spiritual leaders today promote the prosperity gospel by equating grief to self-pity and suggesting that we can exchange trust in God for our authentic experiences of loss.

All of this rests precariously on the dualistic certainty that feeling sad and being happy always and inevitably oppose each other. But is this really so?

I met a woman last year who lost her sixteen-year-old son to cancer. She told me that she feels such tremendous loss in his absence that living actually hurts—a feeling to which I can directly relate. As we began our work together, though, she also told me that she was beginning to feel, at the very same time, a remarkable sense of gratitude for every second she'd spent with him.

For some, it may seem strange to speak of feeling grief and gratitude simultaneously.

For others, if we can set aside the pursuit-of-happiness zeitgeist, this is unadulterated truth.

I assert that being happy does not mean we do not feel pain or grief or sadness—successively or, often, simultaneously. Sorrow and contentment, grief and beauty, longing and surrender coexist in the realm of sameness. This is called the unity of opposites, and it liberates us from a myopic, dualistic view of our emotions as *either/or*.

We are not either happy or sad. We are not either grieving or grateful. We are not either content or despairing. We are *both/and*.

In early grief it is hard if not impossible to imagine ever being happy again, and yet, slowly, moments in touch with joy accrue by seconds and minutes and, later, hours or even days of contentment. Gradually, we regain the capacity to feel joyful, and we feel this in the same space as grieving. Even in moments of joy or lightness, we still know grief—because there is always this ongoing longing for our loved one, for their voice, for their hug, for their touch, for their simple presence. We may also feel grateful for what we have even as we experience despair over what we've lost.

It's so easy to buy into the lies our death-denying culture sells about the pursuit of happiness. And when we do, we find ourselves decrying and resisting painful emotions.

Much of the work I do with those grieving is devoted to counteracting this message, shifting an *either/or* understanding to a more accepting, nondualistic one.

Beauty and pain coexist. But when we are in the early phases of grieving, in order to eventually see beauty in the world again, we must first feel and inhabit our pain. As we do this work, we begin to notice how we move in and out of these seemingly binary states. We needn't eschew grief to be happy, and we needn't decry happiness in order to feel grief. This is a trap of the dualistic mind, and it is life-limiting rather than life-affirming.

Any joy I experience throughout life is not contingent on things going my way, on having no losses, no disappointments, and no (more) deaths. Most important, it's not dependent on forbidding grief to come and go as I know it will for the entire duration of my own life.

Living into this means accepting whatever we feel, moment by moment, without trying to change it. In this way we gradually come to experience a peace with what *truly* is.

THE DEATH-DENYING, GRIEF-DEFYING Cult of Happiness is propagated by messages and mores that value economics over philosophy, productivity over kindness, joie de vivre over authenticity, arrogance over humility, avarice over meaningful human connection, and the egoistic agendas of self-proclaimed healers over what should be commonplace compassion.

This has grim effects for the vulnerable bereaved, further shaming them into hiding.

When this happens, we grievers become masters of dissimulation. When others or we ourselves judge our grief as bad or excessive or going on too long, we feel shame that slumps into repression. If others cannot bear witness to our pain, we learn we must hide it—and even imagine we should not be feeling it in the first place. As evidenced by the response we get from others, we conclude our suffering is quite literally *intolerable*. In seeking to prematurely end justifiable and necessary suffering, we add to it unjustifiable and unnecessary suffering. The danger of trying to bypass grief is that grief then comes out sideways, only now unrecognizable as a legitimate product of loss. In the words of the existential psychotherapist Irvin Yalom, "The pain is there; when we close one door on it, it knocks to come in somewhere else." Or as the poet Rumi puts it, "Some torn places cannot be patched."

The fundamental problem is that grief will wait for us—especially traumatic grief—though if asked to wait too long it often changes form, sometimes becoming toxic and poisoning our very souls.

Seeking only the "good" emotions and avoiding the "bad" emotions is problematic even for those not suffering the death of a loved one. Cutting ourselves off from any genuine feeling in order to pursue or manufacture another feeling denies our humanity. When we reclaim what belongs to us—the pain of our grief, for instance—then we need no longer feel acrimony toward it, and we need no longer expend our valuable energy trying to be rid of that which we wish were not ours. We can simply—or complicatedly—*let it be*.

Whatever comes, we let it be as it is. When we do this, we come to see, in this moment or the next, our emotions always moving. The word *emotion* has its roots in the Latin *movere* and *emovere* meaning "to move through" and "to move out." Our emotions move in us, move through us, and move between us. And when we allow them to move freely, they change, perhaps scarcely and perhaps gradually—but inevitably.

This is grief's most piercing message: *there is no way around—the only way is through.*

11

Bypassing Grief, Bypassing Love

You think your pain and your heartbreak are unprecedented in
the history of the world, but then you read. It was books
that taught me that the things that tormented me most were
the very things that connected me with all the people
who were alive, or who had ever been alive.

—JAMES BALDWIN

A FRIEND OF MINE, Jenny, is a civil engineer who worked for an engi-
neering firm. She would complain about her boss, a man who drank
to excess and who seemed to lack empathy for his employees. Employees experienced him as rude, uncaring, and cold. His wife also drank
too much, and on several occasions, the administrative assistant at the
office had to call a taxi because both of them were too impaired to
drive home safely. Attrition at the company was, unsurprisingly, an
issue; only one employee, the accountant, had been with the company
longer than one year. Though the boss and his wife were an affluent
couple, they never gave employees bonuses or holiday gifts—or even
expressions of gratitude. During the holidays, my friend wanted to
take up a collection of used winter clothes to distribute to the homeless
in their neighborhood, but her boss forbade it with judgmental gen-
eralizations about the impoverished. Jenny was so enraged and saddened by this that she began looking for alternative employment. She
had never experienced such greed, detachment, and cold-heartedness.

She confided her frustration and resolve to leave the company to
the accountant, as the one long-term employee a person who, it turned
out, also knew the owner's secret history: just after the accountant

began working there eight years earlier, the boss's young son had died of leukemia. According to the accountant, the boss hadn't always been this way, and neither he nor his wife had abused alcohol when she was first hired. Their son's death had unraveled them as a family and as individuals. Moreover, the accountant said she had never once seen either of them tearful during or after his death. They took down the son's photos from the office; it was as if he never existed. Their hearts, fearful and shattered, hardened as their lives were suspended by unintegrated grief.

To bypass grief, we must also bypass love. We, as modern humans, are experts in bypassing grief and trauma, cutting ourselves off from pain. Fear drives bypass—curtailing authentic feelings—and bypass leaves us psychologically imprisoned by our own fear. Then we become too frightened to allow our love to flow out, and we build high walls around our hearts to self-protect. In so doing, though, we cut ourselves off from humanity—our own and everyone else's—just as Jenny's boss and his wife had done. Somewhere in our hearts many of us recognize this truth.

Still our culture desperately clings to "closure." We want to wrap grief in a bow and send it off on its way, anywhere else but in the here and now.

It wasn't always this way—and it need not continue to be this way.

WHEN I AM TEACHING LEADERS in the spiritual community, I often remind them that spirituality is a way *into* suffering, not the way out of it. When teaching those in the medical and mental health communities, I remind them that their own terror may get in the way of loving or caring for the grieving person. I ask them to imagine that it is their child or partner or parent who has died—though many decline to take up this invitation; imagining it is simply too terrifying. But if this imaginal exercise proves too distressing to even *contemplate*, what must it be like to live it as reality? In my role as a professor of therapists-in-training, I remind students that they are not unlike their own clients. Because they love, they will experience grief. Many had never considered the possibility of sameness in this regard. The fundamental feel-good chasing that occurs in religious, social, medical, and educational communities permeates public attitudes toward grief.

Mystics in many spiritual traditions see suffering as necessary, essential, the only means toward closeness to God or to existential transcendence. Yet in our medicalized world, normal bereavement and trauma are turned into mental disorders with diagnostic codes, which then become treatable with medications. But if grief is a disease, so too must be love.

I recently worked with a grieving mother who told me that I was her "last chance" at life. Over and over, providers had pathologized her, telling her that she was mentally ill, specifically diagnosed with major depressive disorder and post-traumatic stress disorder. What does "mentally ill" really mean in the aftermath of losing two children and her husband in a fire? She told me tears come nearly every day, even seven months after their deaths. She wonders what she might have done differently to save their lives. She sits in their rooms some days, and other days she can't bear to even walk past those rooms. All of those reactions are *normal* and human. Clinically speaking, I would be more concerned about someone who did not experience some version of those feelings.

The pathological response comes from the culture, in the form of the message that she needs to stop feeling profound grief in reaction to such a profound loss. A society that prevents a woman from grieving for her children and husband as intensely as necessary and as long as necessary is a culture that promotes bypass.

In a certain sense, I suspect the bypassing of traumatic grief may be the greatest threat facing humankind today, responsible for immense suffering from addictions and abuse to social disconnection and perhaps even war. When we disconnect from our grief, we disconnect from ourselves. When we disconnect from ourselves, we disconnect from others and from the natural world. It is an insidious cycle of unnecessary suffering that pervades families, communities, cultures, and generations. By trying to circumvent suffering, we magnify it.

And if we bypass long enough, as individuals or families or cultures, we begin to fragment. When this happens, our emotional range contracts and shrinks—and so does our world.

In *Bringing Home the Dharma,* Jack Kornfield wrote that when he arrived at Ajahn Chah's monastery, the teacher said to him, "I hope you're not afraid of suffering." Jack asked him what he meant and explained that he had come to meditate and find peace and happiness.

"There are two kinds of suffering," Ajahn Chah told him, "the suffering we run from because we are unwilling to face the truth of life and the suffering that comes when we're willing to stop running from the sorrows and difficulties of the world. The second kind of suffering will lead you to freedom."

12

Intensity and Coping

Nature does not hurry, yet everything is accomplished.
—LAO TZU

WHEN I WORK WITH A BEREAVED PERSON one-on-one, I have no "goals" or clinical objectives; I have no "treatment plan" for our time together. I do not try to induce a reduction of symptoms or a diminishment of grief. I have no agenda with my clients other than to be with them as they move with and between and through grief. In this way, there is no need to rush toward any goal, no need to move along to any particular destination. If I play any role at all, the most significant thing I can do is to help them feel the complete, unedited version of their particular story, in the context of their family and in the context of their culture.

Then, rather than bringing their subjective appraisal of grief down, I help them increase their ability to cope. It's an integrative assessment that looks something like this:

Grief intensity (1 least, 10 most)

| 1 | 2 | 3 | 4 | 5 | 6 | 7 | 8 | 9 | 10 |

Ability to cope with grief (1 least, 10 most)

| 1 | 2 | 3 | 4 | 5 | 6 | 7 | 8 | 9 | 10 |

This tool serves to highlight the fact that there are two separate things at play: what we feel and how able we are to cope with what we feel.

If I am feeling a maximum grief intensity of 10 on a particular day—for example, Cheyenne's birthday—but my ability to cope is a 9, also very high, there is only a little tension between what I feel and what I trust I am able to feel from a place of being with what is.

If I am feeling a grief intensity of 6 (medium-high) and my ability to cope is only a 2 (quite low), this discrepancy may give rise to intense distress and psychological disquiet. At such times, I am likely to mistrust myself with my own emotions and, consciously or unconsciously, choose to "check out" by whatever means are readily available.

Within this model, the intention is not to cause the first number (grief intensity) to go down, but rather to allow the second number (ability to cope with grief) to go up. This perspective allows grief intensity to rise and to fall anywhere on the scale naturally, changing and fluctuating—as it inevitably will—in accordance with times and conditions.

From this perspective, the focus is on strengthening our personal and interpersonal resources rather than diluting the many colors of grief. This is crucial because the course of grief, once past the acute period, is to emerge and reemerge, moving from the foreground to the background, rising and falling.

One day, grief may be a 1 or a 2. But most certainly, even years later, there will be days when the intensity will rise again to the higher end of the spectrum. If we cannot trust our ability to cope with the uninhibited rise and fall of grief, we will likely find it increasingly more difficult to tolerate our emotions, relying instead on the distractions that can easily become addictions when the intensity of grief flares up.

Like love, grief can't be constrained by time and space.

Like the rest of the natural world, grief has its own organic rhythm, its own pulse of change.

All we have to do is feel it.

13

Contraction and Expansion

All the beauty of this world is wet with the dew of tears.
—THEODOR HAECKER

GRIEF IS A PROCESS OF EXPANSION AND CONTRACTION.

The expansion-contraction model is seen throughout the natural sciences from astrophysics and cellular biology to thermodynamics and chemistry. As an aging supermassive star runs out of fuel, it begins contracting. That contraction, occurring gradually, may ultimately lead to a dramatic expansion—a supernova. Childbirth is another example of this process: without contractions a child cannot be born. Contractions are excruciating, indescribably painful, yet productive inward movements that combined with an expansion of the cervix are essential to the birth.

The process of contraction and expansion in grief takes place over and over again. Within this model, contraction is not *wrong* or *bad*; contraction need not be halted or controlled. Contraction is necessary for expansion—and thus, contraction is itself part of expansion.

A contraction of grief occurs when our attention and energy are pulled inward, our surroundings made smaller perhaps because, in this particular moment, we feel overwhelmed. Feeling overwhelmed, we contract and tighten emotionally; we conserve our energy and attention, focusing intently on grief—and on self. In a moment of contraction, it feels as if our very survival may be in question. We may feel unsteady, unsafe, unheld; we may feel tenuous, desperate, fearful, and vulnerable. In such moments, we may curl up and hold our breath. In such moments, we feel the call to self-protect. We sense, on some level, that contraction will save us.

Expansion may come with the deep in-and-out breath, in a period of small, even minuscule, growth post-contraction. Allowing contraction to just be, in time we see it naturally ebbs, and the tightness loosens, we grow larger, and we become more willing to venture out and explore, to take risks, to open and unfold. And we find ourselves in a moment of trust, safety, curiosity, willingness, connectedness, belonging—and maybe even hope.

In previous moments, the contraction saved us; in this moment the expansion will save us.

In this model, expansion, too, is not *wrong* or *bad* (or *good* and *right!*); expansion, too, need not be halted or controlled. The expansion, too, is necessary for the next contraction—and thus, expansion is itself part of contraction.

ROLAND'S WIFE SUSAN and only son, an infant, were killed in an automobile accident only four months before we met. Roland, a shy and understated engineer in his forties who married late in life, was understandably devastated. He rarely made eye contact in our first few meetings. Most often his head hung down, and as he spoke, his words were mumbled, barely perceptible.

Then, around the six-month mark, Roland came in feeling lighter. A few days earlier, he'd reconnected with some old friends. They'd asked to see pictures of his baby, Jackson. Everyone could see how much he had looked like Roland. He described feeling both heart-broken and heart-warmed as others talked to him about his son. That night, Roland went home and put his wedding pictures back on the walls of the bedroom he had shared with Susan. He watched Jackson's birth video.

This session was the first time he maintained eye contact with me in the many hours we'd spent together.

"I think I might make it," Roland said, with a tinge of hope.

Six months later, near the one-year anniversary of Susan and Jackson's death, Roland and I met in my office. Roland's face, drawn and sullen, expressed what his words could not. "I don't know how to live anymore," he said, speaking the truth of that moment. "My whole life is gone. I've lost it all. Why should I be here?"

I asked him what it felt like to not want to be here.

"Everything has lost its meaning. Everything in my world lost its color. Nothing tastes good . . . a few months ago I thought maybe I was making progress . . . now, I'm in a hole, a tiny little hole, a closet. I feel just the way I did in the first few months. I just want to run away."

We talked for more than an hour about running away and about that tiny, contracted closet of pain. I asked if he could stay with it until it changed.

"What if it doesn't change?" he said, sounding almost panicked.

"It will," I said. "Everything does."

Roland began to make peace with uncertainty in that meeting. Then, after a few weeks, he began to notice that he felt lighter again, and that the door of that tiny, contracted closet of pain was cracking open.

We worked together for almost three years, and Roland started to be able to see his grief as a series of contractions and expansions. One day, late in our relationship, he shared an epiphany: during a contraction (to which he had now learned to surrender) he only felt safe when he knew that he could talk about what he felt with a safe person. If he didn't feel well-supported through the contraction, if he didn't know someone was on the other side of that closet door, near even if apart, he felt easily overwhelmed by his grief and couldn't tolerate being with it.

About a year after our last meeting, Roland emailed me during a contraction.

Just knowing he could reach out to me helped him feel safe. This contraction, he said, was prompted by an emerging romantic interest in a coworker. As a result of those feelings, he'd sunk into a place of questioning, feeling like he was betraying Susan and Jackson.

Roland came to see me a few times in this period. We would stay with those feelings for a few weeks, watching them intensify and then wane. Eventually, he started to notice a more lasting shift.

Two years later, he married that coworker, a woman named Nancy, in a ceremony that would also venerate Susan and Jackson. Nancy and Roland placed a photo of Susan and Jackson on the altar and had a moment of silence for them at the end of the wedding ceremony.

Roland told me that Nancy's willingness to honor his deceased wife and son expanded their intimacy and connection.

DURING CONTRACTIONS, it is essential to have others who can stand by us—so that when we arrive at the pinnacle of suffering, we can turn and look into the eyes of another's compassion and hold through to the other side. During expansion, it is essential to honor contraction too, to remember contraction, and recall that we have endured many contractions—and will endure yet more.

We may fear that we will experience *contraction only*—that a period of contraction will be permanent, leaving leave us paralyzed with pain for the duration of our lives, fearful of love and life, and terrified of more pain, in a kind of living death. We may long for *expansion only*—a futile endeavor, a phantom, a ruse. Trying to live in expansion only is a state of self-delusion and inauthenticity that will ultimately leave us unsatisfied with our identity, soulless, worn out from persistent pretense.

The natural course of grief, as in the rest of nature, is contraction-expansion-contraction-expansion-contraction-expansion—perhaps endlessly.

Our emotions *move*—within us, through us, and between us.

Disintegration comes first. Reintegration follows.

A contraction allows an expansion.

This is the wisdom of the universe, the wisdom of your body, the wisdom of your heart.

14

The Collision of Love and Loss

I did not know that she could go away, and take our
lives with her, yet leave our dull-bodies behind. . . .
How am I to comprehend this? How am I to have it?
Why am I robbed, and who is benefited?

—MARK TWAIN

MAUREEN LOOKED INTO MY EYES and she knew.

Still, I had to tell her.

She curled into my lap, knees to her chest, in the back of the car sobbing—"No, no, no, oh my god, no!"—between minute gasps of breath, both hers and mine. I held her as tears soaked through my shirt and dripped down the inside of my blouse onto my belly. I was silently weeping as I held her.

Maureen's body, mind, heart, and soul were in a state of dissent as she cried out for her mother. As if nestling in the womb, all eighteen years of her rounded into me as we drove the long ten miles to say farewell to her mother.

I HAD MET MAUREEN'S MOM, Terri, ten years earlier when she moved in across the street from me in Phoenix. We became fast friends, sharing holidays together and late nights talking about philosophy, kindness, love, compassion. I'd even almost converted her to vegetarianism.

Terri volunteered to help the MISS Foundation, in honor of her sister, Carrie, who had died four decades earlier—before Terri was born. When she and her former husband, Mike, had filed for divorce, they were graceful, affable, and cooperative, and they remained close friends for years. I deeply admired the way they cared for one another through the grief of that divorce. Over the course of time, I'd see Terri through many difficult days and nights—some of them the normal struggles of being a newly single mom, some of them related to her own existential questioning. When I moved to Sedona, she'd visit and we'd hike and sit, silently, on the majestic red rocks.

Terri still lived in Phoenix, and one day I happened to be there for a meeting. I texted her to see if she wanted to get together for coffee.

She texted back, "So sorry Jojo, I don't feel well at all. Another time?"

"Oh, no good! Sickies?"

"Yeah."

"No problem, feel better! Love you!"

That was my last contact with Terri.

WHAT I DIDN'T KNOW AT THE TIME was that Terri had been very depressed.

A few weeks earlier she was in California where she'd seen a physician who prescribed multiple psychiatric medications, hoping to stabilize her. But she had instead deteriorated further into despondency, spiraling downward into a vortex of strange and highly uncharacteristic behaviors: akathisia, anhedonia, irrationality, fearful anxiety, and social isolation. This last was even more remarkable because Terri had always been very attached to and reliant upon her small circle of friends. She had become fearful even to see her children.

A month later, I got a call from her former husband: "Jo, Terri died. Suicide. Please call right away. Please call me. Please as soon as you can."

I remember exactly where I was standing when I heard this message. I shook my head. I replayed the message. I walked outside and played it again. In my head, over and over, I was shouting, *"What? What? What!?"*

I called Mike back and rushed out the door to head to the streets of the old neighborhood that held so many years of wonderful memories. I pulled up to Terri's house. There was the familiar crisis-response van, investigators, police.

Mike ran over to me, and we held each other and cried.

We waited until after midnight in the cold desert air, not dressed for such conditions, floating in and out of our bodies. It was nothing short of a nightmare.

Terri had three children—ages twelve, thirteen, and the oldest, Maureen, eighteen. I was the one who told them that their mother had died. Our hearts were breaking together.

I picked up Maureen from a friend's house and drove her home, to the place where her mother had just died. All ten miles of that were excruciating—Maureen quivering with confusion. "I want to see her, Jojo. Please, can I see her?"

"Are you sure you want to do that, sweetie?" I said.

She insisted.

So we waited outside for hours until they wheeled Terri out on the gurney, covered in a thick black blanket. Maureen put her head gently on Terri's chest, and I held her as she sobbed. As is so often the case with trauma, it is hard to know how much time passed as we stood there saying farewell to Terri. I didn't hurry Maureen or suggest she do anything at all.

But when Maureen was ready, she took a deep, gasping breath, lifted her head slowly, placed it ruefully into my chest, and whimpered as they put Terri into the van. She looked up at me and said, "I hurt, Jojo! Oh my heart hurts!"

"Yes, sweet Maureen," I said. "Yes . . ." My heart hurt too.

Though Maureen was a very young woman when her mother died, something in her wise heart affirmed that her pain was a declaration of her love for Terri.

None of us in that house slept all night.

WE DO NOT EXPERIENCE GRIEF WITHOUT LOVE, and we cannot experience the love without feeling grief. When we open our hearts to grief, over time, the delineation between the two states deliquesces. Our hearts open, because grief, like love, is a matter of the heart.

Grief occupies the space between people.

It has its place in the family, at the dinner table and on vacations, in pews and on porch swings.

It occupies time and space, passed along from one generation to the next.

Grief, like love, is open-ended.

Yet in so many people, while love is welcomed and encouraged, grief is stifled and suppressed by fear.

15

Boundless and Timeless Love

I never knew grief felt so much like fear.

—C.S. LEWIS

MONA'S ONE-YEAR-OLD CHILD, Ben, died at home—suddenly and unexpectedly.

Mona was asked by life to bear the unbearable.

She was asked by death to endure the unendurable.

She came to see me one winter morning. It was particularly cold in Phoenix that day—and even though it was forty-five degrees out, Mona was dressed in a tank and shorts.

She began to wail in my office, a visceral howl.

She fell onto the floor, and I moved next to her without interrupting the primal scene. Nearly an hour passed.

"*I can't! I can't* do *this!*" she said.

And so, she didn't. For a while, she didn't come to my office, to the place of her wailing. We spoke on the phone a few times, but I did not see Mona again until May of the next year, just before Mother's Day.

"I'm so sick of it," she said. She was growing weary of the being told what to do, with increasing pressure and insipid platitudes: have another baby, trust in God's will, believe that everything happens for a reason. One person, apparently, even told her she should be grateful that it wasn't one of the older children who'd died.

Such remarks flout the laws of basic human compassion, offering an irrelevant Band-Aid to soothe a gaping, open wound. It was no wonder Mona was feeling increasingly lonely and desperate.

Mona loves her child, thinks of her child, worries about her child, talks to her child, and walks with her child—why should she "get over" that? She recognizes the boundlessness, the timelessness of her bond with her son. She welcomes when others remember Ben—all the while feeling unfathomable grief.

Being a bereaved mother is, perhaps, the hardest job of all and certainly one worthy of recognition on Mother's Day.

That first year, I helped Mona choose a Mother's Day card for herself, one she imagined that Ben would have liked for her. She asked her parents for a charitable donation in honor of Ben. Every Mother's Day to follow, she would remind herself: I am still his mother, as worthy as *any other* mother of recognition.

Sadly, many friends continued to overlook her or were too fearful to approach her with that simple acknowledgment.

I HAD MANY of the same experiences as Mona: insensitive words intended to soothe but which just caused me more pain, filling me with more self-doubt. And yet, I was able to remind myself in my journal: "Sometimes *being* is the only way that I can *be*." Sometimes *being* in grief, or *being* weak, or *being* encased in a womb of pain was the only way I could continue to exist in any form.

The alternative was *ceasing,* becoming my own void—utter nothingness.

And at that time, the prospect of nothingness was the only thing more frightening to me than grief—because if I ceased to exist, I could not continue to bring Cheyenne into the world.

So, instead of trying to be or feel anything in particular, my practice, like Mona's, became just *being* with each moment as it came.

GRIEF CAN BE TERRIFYING.

And why would we not be afraid? Deep in grief, we look up and see the reflection in our mirror is not our own, not us as we have previously known ourselves. We are changed, and we do not recognize the stranger we have become. We long for our old lives, our old selves; we crave meaning and belonging—we ache for them.

The yearning is unquenchable.

And that sense of emptiness propels us toward unsuccessful attempts to fill that person-shaped hole. The distractions we use to take us from our feelings are one way we try to sate that emptiness.

The only alternative to distraction is *being with* grief—one painful, terrifying moment at a time.

16

Personifying Grief

It's typically American to equate healing with *doing*
something. When we have a problem, we fix it, and we
prefer to do it quickly. But fixing is not the same as healing;
in fact it can easily get in the way of healing. . . . Healing
happens not through doing but through feeling.

—ELIO FRATTAROLI

"I NEED YOUR HELP. I don't know if I can live. Please help me!" the
voice on the phone implored. "My husband . . . my husband died. He
was my twin flame. I can't live without him." We made an appointment for the following day.

The next day, the caller, Jennifer, made her way into my office. A
tall, slender, stunningly beautiful woman, she had once been an actor
in Hollywood, and that was easy for me to imagine. Even in her bro-
kenness, her charismatic presence filled the room.

She and her husband of three decades had lived a beautiful life
together until his traumatic death. She would move in and out of
gasping tears, shaking and trembling, fearful that she could not—and
would not *want* to—survive.

It took several meetings for me to begin to understand the dimensions of Jennifer's struggle with grief.

Over and over, we would discuss her tendency toward judging
her tears as "bad" or their absence "good." Sometimes she could cut
through that, and sometimes she would even seem to integrate this
understanding. Then the next day, or several days later, she'd call me
in confusion and despair when her feelings turned "bad" once again.

In our fifth meeting, I invited Jennifer to try what I call a personification exercise: I asked her to create a character, like in a movie script, who embodies what her grief feels and looks like. In our next session, Jennifer returned with quite a story.

SHE INTRODUCED ME TO HELGA, the personification of her grief.

Helga was an old, slumped-over Jewish woman with sparse ashen hair, decaying teeth, withered skin, and an anemic complexion. Helga's clothing was black and tattered, the edges frayed and unhemmed. Helga was "so old and tired and bent over with the weight of grief, it was hard to walk and she just shuffled, not really even picking up her feet."

Helga was collapsing into herself.

Jennifer—a beautiful, strong, and independent woman with a firm internal locus of control—was transforming into Helga: ugly, weak, needy, and out of control. For Jennifer this was a terrifying loss of safety, desirability, and identity. Add to this unease the primary grief of losing her husband Jeff, and it is easy to understand why she consistently felt emotionally pummeled and exhausted.

Jennifer was very good at resisting Helga, but Helga was persistent.

For the next nine months, Jennifer and I—and Helga—collaborated on this project called grief. For the first few sessions after Helga came into our lives, Jennifer would not allow her in our meetings. Instead, Jennifer would document Helga's cruelty, how she came over uninvited, how she broke things, how she destroyed Jennifer's house. One time, Helga barged in on a perfectly lovely time Jennifer was having in New York City. For many weeks, Jennifer continued to resist Helga's trespasses.

Helga's own house, Jennifer told me, was ghastly—icy and dank. Within it, Helga often sat alone in a chair, with the curtains drawn.

One day I asked Jennifer what it might be like if she went over to Helga's house: "What if you set up a time to visit her and have tea?"

At first, the suggestion felt outrageous to her, but Jennifer was curious too and finally agreed to it.

The next week, Jennifer and Helga came to our meeting *together*.

Helga didn't say anything; she just watched and listened. Jennifer told me she'd gone over to Helga's house but couldn't stay there because it was too frightening. But over the next six months, Jennifer and Helga cultivated a relationship. After all, Jennifer said, "Helga knows all the parts of me."

Eventually, Jennifer and Helga were able to sit together at Helga's over tea by the fireplace and get to know one another even better. As Jennifer learned to pause, to feel, to stay with Helga, her fear began to dissipate.

She began to see Helga as less threatening.

One day, Jennifer called me sounding very excited. "Guess what?" she said, "Helga got a makeover!"

Helga was suddenly standing taller, her hair was growing in and the gray fading—she even put on some new clothes and got a facial. As Jennifer was resisting and fearing Helga less, Helga was transforming into a benevolent rendering of Jennifer's grief, an old friend.

When Helga was ready for a change, Jennifer helped her. But first, Jennifer had learned to accept Helga just as she was because it wasn't just the grief that Helga embodied—Helga loved Jeff too.

17

Pausing with Grief

Waking up is not a selfish pursuit of happiness,
it is a revolutionary stance, from the inside out,
for the benefit of all beings in existence.
—NOAH LEVINE

I WAS STANDING IN FRONT of the Alice in Wonderland ride at Disney-land with my three children. A sign read, "Must be at least three years old to ride."

Cheyenne would have turned three that summer.

My heart sank and a dropping feeling in my belly nauseated me. I was frozen with grief. Cameron, my second born, saw the look on my face: "Mommy, are you okay?"

I didn't hear him the first time.

I was fixated on the sign.

My mind ran off with me into thoughts of what should've, would've, could've been: *She should have been here.* We would have had so much more fun if she were here. If only I could have saved her.

Cameron repeated his question snapping me back into the moment.

"Yes, yes," I murmured, "I just . . . well . . . I miss your sister. If she were here, she'd be able to ride this with you." Tears fell from my eyes.

My children looked at me, all three of them, and I apologized.

Of course, they were kind and loving with me. We'd had many open discussions since Chey's death. This was yet another lesson for them, and me, about grief: it follows you.

I missed Cheyenne at home every day of her absence. I missed her while away from home. And I realized that I would miss her for the rest of my life in many forms and under many circumstances.

I asked the children if we could just sit for a minute—and we did.

They were patient with the tears that fell that sunny California day. I allowed myself to stay in the pain of grieving the three-year-old who would ride with her brothers and sister, if only she could, in that moment.

As I paid attention, I noticed the feeling began to slightly lift, that I was ready: "Okay, is everyone set for a ride?"

They looked at each other and at me. I smiled at them, with reddened eyes and reindeer nose. Ari, my eldest, said, "We don't have to go, Mommy."

In that moment, though, I really was ready to take them on the ride.

And so I did, and we laughed—even as I remained aware of her absence and all that she was missing.

Later that day, I went to the Disney box office and anonymously bought a child pass for someone else's little one—not because it diminished my grief, but because I was evoking Cheyenne's love into the world by reaching out to someone else.

I'd had to be with grief before I could do that.

WE PAUSE to *be with* grief, joining the rebellion against a hedonistic culture of happiness-at-all-costs and reclaiming our rightful feelings.

We learn to *just be* without needing to tame, alter, or displace our emotions.

This is radically countercultural, even revolutionary, when all other social forces merge to quell, overcome, and conquer grief. All the while, we renounce the ideas that happiness is something to pursue, a guarantee, an entitlement for every person, and that securing our own happiness is the preeminent purpose of life.

And so once we have emerged from the seismic crisis of loss, what does pausing to *be with* grief look like?

The basic tenets of this revolution are to cultivate self-awareness, emotional transparency, and self-compassion.

Is it painful? Oh, yes—beyond all words.

Yet we slowly learn to stay with our own pain.

We learn we don't have to check out to endure.

The liberating thing about understanding grief this way is that, as with the uniqueness of our fingerprint, every person's "grief-print"— their individual process of *being with* grief—will be different.

There is a wide range of emotions associated with grief, not just sadness and despair. We may become aware of a feeling of loneliness, for example, and, rather than deny, distract from, or repress the feeling, we pause and stay with it because we *see* it.

Seeing it, we are awake and self-aware even amid the ache and unease.

As we watch the emotion, we may notice it starts to change, either intensifying or waning. We notice the change, and we continue to abide with it.

When we've settled in with the feeling, we may notice our resistance relaxing—then we may choose, mindfully, to do something different, like reach out to a trusted friend or hang out with one of our favorite pets or go for a walk. Whatever we decide to do in response to our feeling of loneliness, however, it is done with conscious intention rather than unexamined impulse.

Fully inhabiting painful feelings helps us adjust to and accommodate them. They become more familiar and, while they may not abate, they lose some of their power over us.

Grief is like the monster in my childhood closet: if I can muster the courage to get out of bed and turn on the light, I realize that he isn't so terrifying and may not even be who I believe he is. After going to look at him where he hides, I climb back into bed and confront his gaze again in the darkness. If I repeat this often enough, I even learn to trust him.

I begin to understand that monster isn't separate from me.

He is part of me, part of my mind.

The more we practice staying with the emotions that we think may overcome us, the more we trust our ability to fully inhabit grief. The more we inhabit it, the more comfortable we are staying and allowing it to move through us.

It's a feedback loop that perpetuates self-regard, self-trust, self-compassion, and acceptance of our genuine feelings.

This way of being in the world becomes the crucible, holding space for grief however it shows up in each moment.

18

The Practice of Being With

The healing from the pain is in the pain.

—RUMI

AS GRIEF COMES AND GOES, as we allow our emotions to be whatever they are without having to turn away or supplant them with another contrived feeling, we can express them in many creative, healthful ways. We might do that through reflective practices such as mindful walking, talking, meditation, prayer, reading, gardening, yoga, cooking, hiking, sewing or knitting, building something, by spending time in nature, or by creating art. The creative arts nearly beg for the expression of the ineffable through music, drawing, sculpting, poetry, painting, dancing, storytelling, chanting, drumming, and through ritual and symbols.

Personally, I benefit immensely from element-gazing: watching clouds, seeing the wind stirring leaves, building a campfire and watching the dance of the flames, observing the movement of water in a fountain or a stream, focusing on a patch of earth while contemplating the otherwise imperceptible microscopic movements.

An emotion-focused journal—a diary that documents not what we did that day but how we *felt* that day—is another tool I've used to really turn the heart inward toward grief. I know of one woman who collects stones, each one reminding her of an emotion she's feeling that particular day. Sometimes, she will take them home and paint one side with a color she feels expresses her feelings. Another person collects dragonfly totems, an emotional talisman of her undying connection to her dead son. These tangible representations are a means to externalize the center of our grief.

And unrestrained lamenting itself is a practice, sometimes planned and other times spontaneous.

TATUM, a teenage girl whose mother died of cancer just after she started high school, would bring down her box of special family photos when she wanted to feel close to her. She would play her mother's favorite songs from a list they created together before her death. She knew this would bring her to a place of deep sadness and open weeping, and she welcomed it because she felt closest to her mom during these times, as if her mom were sitting right there comforting her. Tatum intuitively understood that remembering her mom would bring what she called "righteous tears that felt cleansing."

Biochemically, crying may actually act as a stress-relief valve. Emotional tears are different from other types of tears, like irritant tears to dilute or rinse the eye or lubricant tears that support blinking or the elimination of foreign objects. Scientists have found that emotional tears contain 24 percent higher protein concentrations, including adrenocorticotropic hormone. This is a protein produced and then released in high doses during distress that signals the adrenal glands to release hormones that assist in the regulation of stress. Perhaps this is why young children, quite naturally, cry often—as means through which they are able to better cope when feeling frustrated and challenged.

And perhaps this is why Tatum—like all of us—felt calmer and "cleansed" after having a good long cry of remembering.

19

My Heart Cried Many Tears

Our holy place is holy still; our love is not diminished by
absence or by pain. Death has but interrupted our loving,
and I know I shall see you again, if the world lasts.

—NANCY WOOD

IT WAS ABOUT 3 A.M. when I received a desperate email from a Pima woman whose six-year-old son had recently been murdered. Our first communication was through email, and we would continue that way for about a week before we met.

In one of our later exchanges in that period she wrote,

Forever would not be long enough to be with him. That's how I feel about my child, that him being next to me forever wouldn't have been long enough. It seems that every day brings more and more memories that just flood my mind. The cool air in the morning reminds me of waking up and feeling him next to me, oh so close. I would get up and be in the kitchen making French toast, his favorite, and then I would hear him coming down the hallway his feet shuffling on the floor because he was wearing his little sleeper pajamas.

I went to a Powwow today, and I know if he were here he would have been next to me. We used to go to them all over Arizona, North Dakota, New Mexico, and in California. He loved to dance, and our way is to allow children to experience the most powerful, positive tool, the drum. And of course he loved his people. I struggle with this now as I have always looked to my family for strength and now I believe that they are hiding from shame their own grief or disbelief over what has happened to Jacob. This has hurt my heart, but not as much as Jacob's death. My spirit is broken, my heart feels shattered and this moment is unbearable.

I say to you, *Sap and en ta:t mapt am ab ju i:da hen vehejed* (It is good what you have done for me). Touching me as I experienced my deepest emotions. Thank you.

We met in person about a week later when she attended a support group I facilitated. I knew she felt overwhelmed, so I sat close to her. We continued to email daily as she tried to find a way she could feel safe being with her grief. She wrote, "I am struggling very much. I tell you this because I feel like I can trust you." I asked her to tell me about her native burial tradition, the ways in which she wanted to say farewell to her son but because of the circumstances around his murder, she was unable to do.

As part of her work with grief, she wrote this to her dead son a few weeks later:

> Let me say this: they call me Nowch, I am Native, I am Two-Spirited and my heart cries many tears. My name means "beloved friend" in my language. I was taught our traditional ways by my auntie and my *Emo:g* (father). My child, my *a:li* (baby), my precious Jacob, I wish I could have done this the right way for you. I wish I could have made you be settled and made your spirit soar, free from the pain, free from the fear that was shown to you. I wish I could hold you and wipe your tears and tell you how much I love you. I wish you knew that I think of you every second and that I will never let the world forget you.

And writing to me later, she was eventually able to talk about her native tradition:

This is the way it should have been:

I would have stayed with him and taken him to my elders. They would have taught me how to wash my child's body, washing him to ensure that his spirit is safe, free and that his spirit will be protected as his journey continues.

I would have stayed with Jacob until sunrise. I would wrap Jacob in his burial blanket and our Holy Man would come and bless him, smudge his body, smudge my body. Precious, precious baby of mine, I crave your smile, your laughter. I crave your arms around my neck. I feel your heartbeat.

Our burial is simple . . . dirt. As we all come from *jived* (land/earth), we all need to return. No headstone. Traditional songs, honor songs for you. I can hear the drums, feel the beat, and hear the strong words of your honor deep in my heart.

None of this happened . . . this is why I am troubled in many ways . . .

So I need to find my own way to come to peace with what has happened. This seems impossible. Today is difficult. Today I cry many, many tears. Today I am very sad. I wonder what will become of me. I wonder if I will survive the loss of my beloved child . . .

They call me Nowch Hasik. I am Native, I am Two-Spirited and my heart is broken.

I DID NOT TRY TO HEAL HER or change her or offer a solution to the unsolvable.

Nowch and I worked together for years, still to this day, in radically traditional ways, the *real* traditional ways: ceremony, retreat, and storytelling became powerful means of being with grief. On her own, according to her native tradition, Nowch carves gourds, creates spirit sticks, and writes poignant poetry as a way to be with grief and invoke her son.

Here is one poem she wrote Jacob:

THE MAKING

As my hands wrap this leather around this wood

I remember your hand in mine . . . fingers entwined with mine . . .

and do you know I would jump across to the other side if I could
  catch you . . .?

These four directions that I raise my hands to . . .

these clouds that I stare at . . . the wind that brushes across my
  skin . . .

it must be you . . .

and do you know I would jump across to the other side if I could
  catch you . . .?

I hear your voice in the water that rushes by . . .

I see your reflection in the sun that shines in my eyes . . .

the beauty of it all brings me to my knees . . .

and do you know I would jump across to the other side if I could
  catch you . . .?

The moon is shining for you and the stars light up the sky . . .

as I wrap your four directions into my soul . . .

and do you know I would jump across to the other side if I could
  catch you . . .?

ABOUT THREE YEARS AGO, Nowch gave me a spirit stick she made from wood near the river by the cemetery where Jacob is buried. She also buried another spirit stick on the day of Jacob's burial and disinterred it on the one-year anniversary of his death.

The spirit stick she gave me is wrapped in cord, representing each of the four directions, beaded symbolically, and it is honorably displayed so that I, too, remember Jacob with her.

20

The Barefoot Walkabout

Sharp knives seemed to cut her delicate feet,
yet she hardly felt them—
so deep was the pain in her heart.
—HANS CHRISTIAN ANDERSEN

WHEN I WANT TO BE WITH MY GRIEF, I hike barefoot into the mountains, usually alone and in silence. I found this practice in 2007 when I was hiking up Brewer Trail near my home in Sedona. I'd had a stressful week and felt on edge, my mind discursive.

The day prior, I'd been in contact with eight families whose children had died. The grief moved through my body—it was palpable—and I felt my own sense of despair for the agony I knew they suffered: an agony for which there was no cure, no verse, no healing I could perform. I knew I needed to get into nature.

The magic of the natural world has always awed me.

But on this day, the superficial distractions of my mind taking me away from my own potent feelings of shared grief were powerful enough to disconnect me from my emotions. Disconnected, I no longer felt angst about the too-many-grieving families I'd met the day before, but I also missed every bird's song. I missed the clouds and the rising sun. I missed the manzanita and the little daisy growing between the spines of the saguaro.

It was as if I wasn't even there at all. Before I realized it, I'd hiked almost two miles to the top of the trail but had no memory of the journey there. Preoccupied and out of my body is not a way I want to live my life. So I decided that I would emulate the discalced Carmelites of the fifteenth century and hike barefoot down the trail.

This practice, which I use about monthly, teaches me to stay present even when the present moment hurts.

It teaches me that I can feel grateful for a cool, smooth stone on the path.

It teaches me that I can avoid the cactus needles when I pay attention—and that rocks between my toes hurt.

It teaches me that though I cannot always see around the next corner, I trust myself on this path.

It teaches me that sometimes I can lean on the unexpected, like the titan juniper pine I'd walked past many times but never *really* saw.

And it teaches me that I cannot provide shade for myself—only another being can provide shade for me.

My barefoot hiking practice, rich in metaphors, is a compelling medium for me. While it's not for everyone, many others I've worked with have also integrated various aspects of it as part of their own practice.

For me, walking barefoot is a way of being with grief.

21

The Vitality of Self-Care

Grief is love turned into an eternal missing. . . .
It can't be contained in hours or days or minutes.
—ROSAMUND LUPTON

WHEREVER WE ARE IN OUR GRIEF JOURNEY, *pausing* causes us to land on the self.

The focus is very much turned inward. Grief, particularly traumatic grief, is a wound to the self. When we are deeply wounded, we *must* turn our focus to the injured place in order to survive.

A few years ago, I met with a young father, John, who had lost his son in an accident. His son died in the United States while John was in military combat overseas. Imagine his sense of helplessness being thousands of miles from home and getting the news of his son's death. John described his return stateside—and the texts, telephone calls, and flights that went with it—as surreal, dreamlike.

The first few months, John focused only on his wife and rejected others' compassion when directed at him. Not attending to his own grief, over time he began to drink heavily. He lost his job and nearly his marriage.

It was the concern over his marriage that brought him to me.

When we talked about the early events of his son's death, John told me that he had been too scared to let himself feel the pain early on and that he'd been drinking and having extramarital affairs since his son's death.

When we talked about early traumatic grief as a *wound*, he understood that in the context of his own military service: "If I had encountered an IED in the field that exploded and I lost my legs or arms, I would *have to* focus on myself." Yes, he understood—he got that self-focus could be honorable and appropriate. Grieving, he had to attend to his own wounds—perhaps foremost. And ultimately, when we take good care of ourselves, we are better able to take care of others. Far from being selfish, in a way self-care in acute grief is heroic.

This is the place of heart-turned-inward.

ATTENDING to the self-focused, self-caring place of heart-turned-inward doesn't mean we stay in that place, always and forever. That, too, changes. We will move, vacillating between self and other, heart-in and heart-out, over time.

What this means for grievers is that we may have what I call *re-grieving* days, days when acutely experienced grief reemerges months, years, or decades later on a special day, holidays, or without any particular cue or prompt. On re-grieving days, grief moves to the foreground again, and we may feel weepier than usual, tenderhearted, and vulnerable.

When we notice that foregrounding of grief, it's okay to turn our hearts inward and focus on that moment—in fact, it's essential. And when we do that, we're also reminded of the need for self-care.

Self-care is crucial for those who are grieving.

Its necessity is nonnegotiable.

Disconnection from our emotional world can cause a disconnection from our physical world and vice versa. Emotions are not merely isolated mental sensations; emotions influence physical sensations, mental cognition, social exchanges, existential howling, and even how we feel about how we feel.

Some people with whom I've worked are concerned that self-care is self-indulgent. Reframing that view, I use the example of being very sick with the flu. Suffering from such an illness, I'm going to get into bed, rest, withdraw my energy from the external world, and drink Symfre tea to boost my immune system. I'm going to draw the curtains, pull up the covers, and give myself the time I need to heal.

And others will also need to give me time: they may need to expect less of my attention to go to my usual family tasks, they may need to walk quietly around the house so as not to disturb my rest. They will need to offer provision for my healing. I do my part, and they do theirs.

Self-care is not a selfish act; it is an act of generosity for self and others.

22
Self-Care and Sleep

I wish I could show you when you are lonely or in darkness
the astonishing light of your own being.

—HAFIZ

MANY OF US HAVE GREAT DIFFICULTY allowing ourselves to love or care
for the self. One bereaved mother put it this way: "I don't feel worth
my own love. I feel tremendous guilt, and that guilt gets in the way
of the way I feel about myself. Why should I be compassionate to me
when my child is dead?"

Another woman I worked with after her husband's murder noted
that she believed she was undeserving of love, of self-care, because she
lost the love of her life and she could never allow herself to experience
that again. Part of the work of grieving involves trying to remain conscious of the stories we tell ourselves and then slowly moving toward
active self-care, even in small ways, when we are able.

Self-care can take many forms: eating well, getting a massage,
exercising, finding solitude, being surrounded by loving others, and
getting enough sleep.

Sleep is paramount to our well-being. When we have not slept
soundly, think about how intolerant and impatient we become, how
stressed or hungry or exhausted we are. Consider the effects of the
lack of sleep on cognition, problem solving, memory retention, and
even our sense of balance.

Good sleep hygiene will not, of course, alleviate grief (nor would
we want it to!)—but it will help us better cope with our fluctuating
emotional states.

Kim's daughter, Kathy, had died eight months before our first meeting.

Kathy was a vibrant young woman who had just married a year earlier and was looking forward to starting her own family. She was only twenty-seven years old. She died following a routine surgical procedure.

Kim, like so many others, expressed a strong desire to be rid of grief. Yet she also wanted to be able to invoke Kathy's beauty and their shared love, but when she tried to access those feelings, which she labeled as "good," the feelings she labeled as "bad" would overtake her.

So she engrossed herself in work, in activities. She tried happiness retreats, meditation retreats, empowered women retreats. She tried churches of every branch, sect, and denomination. She tried various traumatic grief therapies with the distinct purpose of circumventing grief. And through all this her downward spiral was swift.

The grief persisted, presenting and re-presenting itself in many forms and in odd moments that would catch her off guard. Kim's sleep suffered intensely. She stopped reaching out to friends, even those who were capable of compassionate listening. She self-medicated with alcohol, and that made it more difficult for her to function at work. She lost weight. And she began to feel a pressing sense of loneliness overcoming her.

During our first meeting much of her focus was on how to bring her grief to an end. I asked her, "What does that feel like? What does it feel like to want something to end so badly, but it just seems like it won't?"

"I can't think of anything else. It taunts me," she said. "Grief taunts me."

During the next few weeks, we would gradually work on allowing the "bad" emotions to be what they were while not grasping at the "good" emotions. She began to notice that the more she avoided being with her grief, the more unendurably taunting it became. And she noticed that the more unendurable the grief became, the less connected she felt to herself and to Kathy. Kim began to realize that she had abandoned her own deep knowing, her intuitive calling to remember Kathy *in toto*—good and bad. That meant, for Kim, sheltering all the feelings and memories—not forcibly recalling only the "good" and not forcibly pushing away all the "bad."

Slowly, as we began learning to pause together, to be with grief, Kim started to feel more capable of listening to the wisdom of her own heart. We cultivated a self-care practice based on her individual needs and interests, and this felt transformative and liberating to Kim.

Once she was able to focus on and allow her genuine emotional experiences, bringing attention to her holistic needs and caring for herself came more naturally—in a way she described as painful but life-affirming.

Over the next few months, we worked together on her being with grief and self-care practice. Together, we made a plan that looked like this:

1. Getting between 7 and 8 hours of sleep a night, ideally asleep by 10 p.m.
2. Limiting caffeine, nicotine, and other stimulant intake after 3 p.m.
3. Limiting television in the evening; reading a good book instead.
4. Abstaining from alcohol too close to bedtime (or at all).
5. Abstaining from large meals after 7 p.m.
6. Exercising during the day and avoiding day naps.
7. Getting sufficient sunlight during the day (20 minutes).
8. Calming yoga in evening to help relax.
9. Water meditation in a warm bath in the evening.
10. Acupuncture.

11. Maintaining complete darkness. Never sleeping with lights, radio, or television on.
12. Upon needing to use the bathroom in the middle of the night, minimizing light exposure by using a flashlight.
13. Buying a sound machine.

WITHIN TWO WEEKS, this simple list helped Kim move from sleeping intermittently for only three or four hours a night to sleeping six to seven hours uninterruptedly. And not only was she better able to cope with the rise and fall of her grief, but her memories had more clarity and she felt less scattered and reactive.

She also began a moderate exercise regime that included getting out into nature. She noticed she'd often cry on her hikes, feeling Kathy's absence very strongly during those times, yet she learned to trust herself with those feelings, even when their arising seemed paralyzing. She even started eating organically grown vegetables from her new garden—named "Kathy's Place."

Kim's new way of caring for herself also became a way she spent time with Kathy. In this way, she was able to connect with a deeper sense of Kathy's impact on her life.

23

Ways to Care for Yourself

To embrace suffering culminates in greater
empathy, the capacity to feel what it is like for
the other to suffer, which is the ground for
unsentimental compassion and love.
—STEPHEN BATCHELOR

WHEN CHEYENNE DIED, I had a very hard time taking care of my physical body.

I'd been a vegetarian since I was seven years old and was always very cautious about eating "clean"—what I call eating healthfully. While I never went back to eating meat, I found myself not eating at all, or when I did eat, I was not eating healthful food. My weight dropped to barely ninety pounds.

I started to journal my feelings, and I realized through writing that the animosity I felt toward my body was an expression of my emotional pain, primarily the guilt I felt over Cheyenne's death.

Once I became conscious of this, I started to watch those feelings of hostility without judging them. I wrote about my body as a vessel that carried Cheyenne. I asked myself if I would be willing to care for her vessel better, and I created a list that incorporated being with grief with my own self-care practices. It was one way in which I recognized the nobility of my own emotions. I've come to call this practice *becoming one's own hero*.

Here is the encouragement I offered myself:

Dear Joanne,

Please remember to

Have a good cry when you need one.

Drink plenty of water.

Connect with compassionate others.

Accept and embrace emotions without clinging to them,

even the good ones.

Find the sun every day.

Learn to love solitude.

Serve others every opportunity you can.

Sleep seven hours a night.

Eat clean.

Play dirty (get in the mud, walk barefoot, sweat).

Remember your precious dead.

Feel grateful but don't force gratitude.

Notice nature.

Try new things.

Pray and/or meditate.

Find your special song.

Seek out those who made a difference in your life and tell them.

Build bridges between people.

Take a media break.

Treat yourself to a day of comfort.

Rescue an animal.

Buy a stranger a cup of coffee, or tea, or lunch. Anonymously.

Start over again.

With love, I'm trying,

Yourself

SOME OF THE PEOPLE with whom I work make their own list of ways to engage in self-care.

One woman who tragically lost her husband to murder created a list of self-care ideas that was based on her available time. As a corporate executive who worked many hours per week, time seemed a significant barrier in her regimen of taking care of herself. So her self-care list included items that could be done in only a few minutes: stretch, watch clouds, doodle, read a poem, write a thank-you note, just sit. If she had five to ten minutes, she might listen to music, dance in her office, cry or laugh, sing, take a short walk, write a haiku, make a cup of special tea, journal, meditate or pray, clear her space, color, or take a photograph that captured how she felt. If she had thirty minutes, she might also meditate or pray, exercise or do yoga, connect with another person over tea, start a new book, get into nature, do something kind for someone else, clean out a drawer, make art, or send a family member a loving letter.

A grieving father and husband started a "once-a-day vow" practice that he changes once a month. Note that June is the month when his teenage son died:

January: Once a day, I vow to learn something new.
February: Once a day, I vow to do something I enjoy.
March: Once a day, I vow to spend more time outdoors.
April: Once a day, I vow to express my love more openly.
May: Once a day, I vow to call a friend.
June: Once a day, I vow to cry. And smile.
July: Once a day, I vow to go to bed by 9 P.M.
August: Once a day, I vow to read.
September: Once a day, I vow to drink more water.
October: Once a day, I vow to eat more salad.
November: Once a day, I vow to be thankful for the food I have to eat.
December: Once a day, I vow to do something kind for someone.

Another way to create your own practice is to break self-care down into categories. I suggest the following broad areas to attend to: self-expression, self-awareness, connection and interconnection, physicality, and kindness.

Self-expression is about the ways in which we show our feelings. Self-awareness is about the ways in which we begin to pay attention, notice, and listen deeply to all aspects of self.

Connection and interconnection are about the ways in which we are present with others, animals, nature, the world, and even ourself.

Physicality is about tending to our bodily health, paying attention to sleep, nutrition, exercise, dance, and even, when ready, play.

Kindness is about bringing love to others, and we cannot bring love to others without bringing it back around to ourselves—it's a symbiosis and a wonderful way to care for our own hearts.

24

Telling Family and Friends What We Need

> She was a genius of sadness, immersing herself in it,
> separating its numerous strands, appreciating its subtle
> nuances. She was a prism through which sadness
> could be divided into its infinite spectrum.
>
> —JONATHAN SAFRAN FOER

THERE IS NO QUESTION that, for many, grief and the sense of isolation and loneliness amplifies during special occasions, like baby showers, graduations or weddings, and on holidays.

One grieving mother with whom I worked couldn't tolerate baby showers, even years after the death of her newborn son. She described it like this: "I tried going to one shower . . . my sister's . . . to save family harmony. But I found myself thinking of my own son, how it would be to have him here, imagining him as a toddler now, and I felt so alone and empty . . . I had to leave in tears. I felt like people could see through me, like they knew I was the 'bad luck' of new moms . . . it was unbearable." And so, for her, saying she was not going to baby showers until she felt more ready was a perfectly acceptable act of caring for herself.

Self-care also means saying *no* when necessary. When grieving, we need to give ourselves permission to put our own needs first for a while.

It is okay, perhaps even necessary, to turn down invitations to events, cut back on holiday celebrations and the seemingly obligatory decor, and it's okay to ask for help with child family members who may also be grieving. Stress often increases during special occasions, and this naturally distracts us from self-care. Being aware of this tendency to neglect ourselves can help us in staying more vigilant. It's the simplest, hardest thing we can do for ourselves: eat nourishing food, drink plenty of water, have a reasonable sleeping and resting schedule, and significantly limit, if not eliminate, alcohol, caffeine, and other drug consumption.

Part of our practice might be thinking through what might feel right to us, a self-care "wish list" to share with others during these times.

Melody lost her baby, Tristan, on Christmas. I met her the next year, the week before his birthday, on December 20. While the rest of the world was celebrating good cheer and reindeers, she was agonizing over what should have been his first birthday.

Often fear gets in the way of others approaching us, and this adds pain to our pain. With this in mind, together we created her personalized list that she sent out to her family.

Melody's Christmas Wish List

1. I wish to share my emotions openly and honestly to help you understand how I feel in this moment. It changes, day-to-day, season-to-season. So ask me to share how I feel when we get together. And if you're wondering, "Should I talk about Tristan or not?" then just ask me what I need today.

2. Rituals are very helpful for me, especially new ones. Help facilitate new rituals for us. A few ideas, for example, include lighting a candle and having a moment of silence at the beginning of our holiday meal, offering a donation to our favorite charity in his name, setting an empty place at the table for him, volunteering as a family in his memory, buying a gift for a child and donating it in his memory.

3. Offer to attend a support group with me. Comment on photos when I share them on social media. You won't make me sadder than I already am; you'll be sharing my sadness with me. And that helps me.

4. Get out into nature with me. Let's take a walk, hike, or just sit outside and *really* talk. But please don't be afraid to say his name.

5. If I do want to be alone, please give me that time without pressure to participate in family activities. Sometimes, I need solitude. If it seems like I want to be alone but you're not sure, just ask.

6. Help me change our family routine if it feels right. From the small things, like changing the music we play when putting up the tree, changing the meals we eat for a holiday, or leaving town for a vacation during the holidays, novelty may relieve some of my stress.

7. If I have to leave early, please respect my decision and don't add to my guilt. But know that this is less likely to happen if I feel like my grief is being seen and held and if others are remembering with me.

In Melody's case, the family collectively decided to move their Christmas celebration from December 25 to July 25, midyear. She loved that she could still celebrate this holiday with family, but at a time when the despair of grief was not so acute year after year.

ONE WOMAN I WORKED WITH, Marta, felt like others avoided her in their small town after her daughter Jane died. Around Christmas, she noticed that even in the grocery store, people would see her cart coming down an aisle, turn around, and, in Marta's words, "run like hell."

Trying to proactively address this issue, Marta and I wrote a letter that she could give to her family and friends in advance of the holidays:

Dear family and friends,

At this time of year, we are struggling without our daughter, Jane, in our home. We know it is frightening, but we'd like to ask you to talk about her with us and to ask how we are really doing when and if you see us around town. We'd like you to remember her in your prayers, and then tell us when you do. We'd like you to consider a donation to one of our favorite charities in her name.

Please send us emails rather than calling us. We find phone calls to be overwhelming right now. We'd appreciate help with meals during the week of Christmas. If you are able to leave a meal at the door, we'd appreciate it. Our friend Mary will be coordinating that for us. Please contact her directly.

Finally, we love to receive cards so please keep them coming. We love hearing your favorite memories of Jane. Thank you. We are grateful for your support, and will need it for many years to come.

25

Self-Care as Distraction

Always go too far because that is where
you will find the truth.
—ALBERT CAMUS

SELF-CARE means attending to our body, mind, and heart in the wake of loss, but we must be careful to not let this become yet another form of distraction—like any other distraction that mindlessly takes us away from painful feelings.

BEN, a young man whose sister was murdered when he was in his early twenties, finally sought counseling almost a decade later. He had become such a master at excessive self-care that he spent a great deal of his monthly budget, and his time, on what *seemed like* self-care. This included frequent purchases of workout equipment, multiple gym memberships, and myriad meetings with trainers. Then, on the ten-year anniversary of his sister's death, Ben noticed that his first impulse was to buy yet more gym equipment.

Throughout the course of our work together, he came to understand that his hyperfocus on his body was a coping tool he'd learned early after her death. During the trial of his sister's murderer, he would use extreme physical exertion to channel his anger toward the man who killed his sister, and that pattern stuck.

A decade later, the practices had become more than a socially acceptable coping mechanism—now they were a distraction to take him away from pain. The problem was that, as with any drug, he kept having to up the ante, buying increasing volumes of equipment and memberships in order to obtain the same heart-numbing effects. Even fellow workout fanatics told him he seemed out of control.

Our work together would center on staying with his suffering and the painful memories—slowly and in a safe environment—and helping Ben learn to engage in balanced self-care that comes from a place of love rather than fear and avoidance.

The first thing we did was to start a feelings/actions journaling practice to develop emotional and behavioral mindfulness.

Over time, Ben started to notice the impulse to distract arise as soon as he recalled any associated painful memory.

Slowly, we were able to short-circuit that automatic process, and he began to learn to be with grief in its most difficult-to-tolerate states.

Eventually, practicing deep self-awareness, Ben was able to stop using his bodily form as a way out of grief. He continued to work out, consciously, because it was good for his health. But he often waited until the also-good-for-him cry had moved through him.

26

Learning, Adapting, and Trusting Intuition

When you come out of the storm,
you won't be the same person who walked in.
That's what this storm's all about.

—HARUKI MURAKAMI

MY PRACTICE WITH GRIEF has brought me to a place where I've come to understand the trinity of self-awareness: learning, adapting, and trusting intuition.

All things become potential teachers when we are paying attention. When this happens, we begin seeing things we've never seen, perceiving even minutia in the natural world and noticing that the rainbow and the storm show up in the same sky. When the darkness of grief descends, our eyes need time to adjust to this condition—to begin to see subtler and more dimly lit presences.

Practicing attentive self-awareness, we may start to see that there is life in a planted seed working hard under the soil. And we may notice that the trees less likely to break are those that are able to sway with the wind.

We may discern that the easy path isn't always the right path.

And everyone and everything can become our teacher.

Children and strangers teach us.

Animals teach us.

When we are truly awake, even an ordinary moment teaches us something.

Grieving itself is a learning process. We learn so much about ourselves in grief—perhaps more than we could ever want to know. The more I learn about grief, the less I fear it, and the more I felt rooted in myself.

Grieving is also a process of adaptation. We find ways to adjust to the life we never expected or wanted.

Grieving hones our intuition. We are listening more deeply, and our senses, in ways different from before our beloved's death, are sharper, the result of having practiced penetrating awareness of self and surroundings. Sometimes we learn to trust our intuition.

Since I was a little girl, I've been drawn to Sedona. My parents, especially my father, loved Sedona, and I spent countless weekends, summers, and vacations in our home here. Sedona is not a town with abounding sources of entertainment or nightlife, other than the magnificent stars that shine so brightly you can almost touch their glow. When I moved to Sedona full-time in 2010, I felt that I'd found my center. I'd come *home*.

The town I loved so much my entire life was named after the wife of one of its founding settlers, one Sedona Schnebly. I didn't know much about her other than that fact until, following an intuitive impulse, I explored an unknown new route to the organic market and found myself in Cook's Cedar Glade Cemetery. I wandered around curiously reading epitaphs, and chanced upon Sedona Schnebly's grave.

I was surprised that she was hidden in this old unremarkable cemetery. Then I noticed that just next to her grave, another grave read:

> **Pearl A. Schnebly . . . beloved daughter,**
> Born November 18, 1899,
> Died June 12, 1905.

I sat on the red dirt of their graves and paid homage in my heart to my fellow bereaved mother and her little girl.

I never made it to the store that day.

Instead, I began my research into Sedona and Pearl.

Pearl, it turned out, was killed in an accident with her horse. Sedona was there, trying helplessly to save her. Sedona's grief must have been unbearable, and I imagine there was little support in the remote and still unsettled Southwest.

As the story goes, Sedona stared out her kitchen window onto the grave of her beloved Pearl every day.

Several months later, the family would flee the area—a decision Sedona's husband made in a desperate attempt to save her from grief.

Sedona Schnebly did not return to the place she so loved until her own burial forty-five years later, as requested, beside her precious Pearl in 1950.

I visit her grave often now to talk to both of them—and I understand even more why this is the only place on earth I want to live.

27

Re-Grieving

The world breaks us all, and afterward
some are stronger in those broken places.
—ERNEST HEMINGWAY

I REMEMBER THE DAY I dared my first laugh after my daughter died.

When I realized what I'd done, I felt like I'd committed an act of desecration: *I'd dared to break into laughter*. I don't recall who caused this act of irreverence or what that person had said or done to prompt it, but I recall that I was in a public place with a few others.

And I'd laughed. Then, as quickly as the sound exited my lungs, I was standing outside of myself in shame.

Smiling, laughing is an act of being alive—but *I* was not alive. I had no right to laugh. I was lingering in the liminal space between the world of the living and the world of the dead; I certainly *felt* dead. I certainly felt broken, but not broken Hemingway-style, not yet stronger in my broken places.

Having laughed, I excused myself with a gasp and went into the ladies bathroom—where I sobbed inside the stall.

I was not ready to smile or laugh again for a long time.

THE DATE WAS JULY 27 when my world fell silent—twenty-one years ago. Twenty-one years is a long time to miss someone. Twenty-one years is a long time to feel and think and wonder about someone you cannot touch, hear, or see.

The time takes on a strange quality: minutes feel like years, years like minutes.

It happened so long ago yet seems like yesterday; it happened yesterday yet feels so long ago.

The love I have for her, my dead daughter, has not waned.

On special occasions, death anniversaries, and sometimes just an ordinary day when the sun is shining and the clouds are floating and the earth is rotating—on a day like any other—a pang will strike my heart, and I feel the collapse of a moment around me.

Not as often as in the early days, not as lasting as in the early days, but still, it comes.

And I surrender because long past the early days, grief's shadow still remains. It lurks and lingers. It is both feared enemy and beloved companion who never leaves.

Grief calls for us to give ourselves back to it.

To remember.

To reclaim.

To re-grieve.

And for all those things, even when they sting, I am thankful.

28

Surrendering and Stretching

Turning toward what you deeply love saves you.

—RUMI

CULTIVATING A PRACTICE OF SURRENDERING means that we intentionally approach grief over and over—at all stages of our lives.

Our awareness of grief's influence is heightened: the presence of our beloved dead's absence undeniable. We come to appreciate that this immense present grief is here because of another period in time when we were together with them. And that time, that precious time, belongs to us.

When we really pause to reflect, we realize that we would not trade those moments of love for *anything*, not even the promise of abated grief from the passing years.

One young man, grieving the rape and murder of his sister, said it this way, "I am in such pain every day. But I know it's because I love her so much. . . . When people talk to me about *recovery*, it's as if they are telling me that I should stop grieving. I won't stop grieving until I stop loving her."

Recovery is a fascinating word—one I generally eschew because of its reductionist connotations. At a certain point in grief, expectations of recovery begin to knock at our doors. Employers, neighbors, family, friends, and concerned others begin to send messages—both subtle and overt—urging us to resume life as usual.

But life is anything but usual after the one we love has died.

We are changed beings even if we have resumed some semblance of a "new normal." When unsuppressed, grief does change over time.

It may become less gripping as we reengage with life and its mundane duties like paying bills, going to work, doing the laundry, and shopping for groceries. All these long-standing tasks of the living have awaited our return. They are necessary and important, and there are serious consequences for not directing our attention toward these day-to-day actions.

The little things, though, can take us away from the things that matter, and difficulties may arise when we use "normal life" to evade grief.

With practice, we can learn how to balance the things of the living with our beloved dead.

Being with grief, we stretch our bodies and hearts until the point of pain.

As with any stretch, maybe we back off just a little, out of necessity and self-care. Over time, as we hold the stretch, reaching our edge, we learn to wait. In this surrender, our muscles give in to the pose. As we repeat the exercise, we surrender more and more deeply into the stretch. Friends, colleagues, family members may call to us to abandon the stretch, because to them it no longer feels necessary.

But on a special day or during a song or a sunset, if we've given up our practice of stretching, we'll feel our muscles tense against this now-unfamiliar sensation, and it seems just as it did long ago: unbearable.

FOR JOANN, mother to Charlotte, surrendering was a challenge.

Little by little, she noticed the ways she distracted herself: reading, watching movies, sleeping, and busying herself in any number of tasks. Often, fear plays a role: "If I choose to surrender, will I recover and be able to still function at the same level as before?" JoAnn reported thinking about Charlotte and her death constantly, "but mostly at a distance." Sometimes she would try to submit to grief—but noticed something always seems to hold her back from fully surrendering. She felt she could "only submit to the loss in small increments."

Almost three years into her grief journey, JoAnn felt she was still in "survival mode."

Still, JoAnn made great strides in her turn toward grief.

Through various meditations we practiced together, she began to imagine specific things about Charlotte, specific moments with her—for instance how Charlotte's hand felt in hers and how Charlotte would snuggle against her in her flannel pajamas as JoAnn stroked Charlotte's leg.

The courage to turn toward the empty place in our hearts, the fierceness it takes to intentionally remember, has profound effects. JoAnn found that when she remembered Charlotte's size, how her flannel pajamas felt under JoAnn's fingers, the gap between Charlotte's palm and her own when they were holding hands, it became a completely tactile experience and she also remembered "exactly how it felt to have a living daughter."

These memories come with pain, of course.

But pain is not the entire story.

JoAnn describes what it's like:

> In those moments, I feel a genuine smile. It is not a big joyful smile, but instead a smile that is more pure, honest, and loving than any I have ever known. But then, the moment quickly fades and I am reminded of her violent death, and my anxiety reemerges. It is a constant reminder that nothing is permanent, but yet somehow it is. Because in those moments she is real.

The invitation to surrender to grief is about the middle path, straddling both worlds—life and death. JoAnn allowed herself to remember Charlotte, without clinging or avoiding, and it came with both pure love and pain.

The conscious choice not to relegate grief to the backyard—where it would be never seen, cared for, or remembered—is courageous.

And a heart that has been expanded by suffering has the capacity to hold even more love.

ZAADII was a beautiful, brown-eyed little boy who loved his family intensely and believed he was a younger version of Batman. His mom, Rachel, was injured in the same accident that killed Zaadii—a reckless driver hitting pedestrians.

Rachel attended one of my traumatic grief retreats only weeks after Zaadii's death. The concept of *being with* grief felt absurd to her at first, but she was eventually able to begin to explore it. And when she did, when fully inhabiting her grief, she could touch the nonduality of love and grief, even if momentarily.

Eight months later, I received this note from her:

> Yesterday I decided to finally do one of the things you told us last summer, to just *sit with* the grief when that wave comes and not just run from it. And it was okay. It actually seemed to hurt less than when I'm trying to escape it. My tears felt warm and strangely beautiful and comforting—still pain in there, but a lot of love too. I felt like Zaadii was in my arms for a moment.
>
> You demonstrate to all of us that we can survive, we can thrive again, and that we can bear what seems so unbearable. That there is no other side, just a new route much more complex and deeper than before but also filled with beauty and appreciation.

BY RE-GRIEVING AND REMEMBERING, we discover the mysterious healing power of staying in the stretch, remaining connected to both the beauty of loving and the pain of having lost. Surrendering requires our steadfast commitment to stand up and turn *toward* grief while living in a culture obsessed with ushering grief, scorned, out the door.

Disconnection from grief fragments our already fragile identity—and protecting that intimate connection to our dead can be, for us, an elixir of life.

29

When We Fragment

But there was no need to be ashamed of tears,
for tears bore witness that a man had the greatest
of courage, the courage to suffer.

—VIKTOR FRANKL

"WHAT AM I DOING HERE?" Lisa asked, nearly three years after Anthony died. Anthony, at age eighteen, had been her only living son. Michael, her firstborn, had died at age twelve, thirteen years earlier. Her eyes implored me to give her a reason to live. "When Michael died, Anthony was my *reason* . . . now Anthony is dead too."

Enduring the death of one child is painful enough.

Now Lisa, twice-bereaved, sat pleading for help.

We started working together only weeks after Anthony's death. She felt she'd never fully grieved for Michael and wanted to "do it right" this time. Early on, she'd attended my grief retreats and support groups and had come to counseling weekly.

Being with grief, as painful as it was, was more fluid than we both imagined.

She'd come off her psychiatric medications, prescribed when Anthony moved away to college, within the first few months after we met. Somewhere around a year and a half after Anthony died, we started working together less frequently as she started reengaging with life.

She and her husband owned a construction company, and she was finding it difficult, if not impossible, to balance living with grieving.

Lisa was only recently in contact with anger—which she identified as *rage*—and reported she didn't "do rage well." Not being comfortable with her strong emotions, she began self-harming trying to "claw out of her own skin"—particularly during marital conflict attributed to her inconsolable grief. During our time together this day, we'd talk about surrendering to grief rather than resisting it and what that might look like.

"I don't know how to stay with it. I don't know how to feel it without fearing that I'll never come back from it," she said.

I asked her to look *beneath* the rage, beneath what happened when she acted out her emotional pain on her physical body. "I think I need my pain to be seen, validated—and I don't think it is," she said tearfully after a long period of contemplation.

A deeply maternal woman, Lisa's love for her boys is passionate, but she was being drawn into the world of the living again and was having great difficulty resolving that tension.

I asked Lisa to pay attention to what happened just before she harmed herself.

She had a sense that she resented when others tried to force her into "moving forward" and she needed a way to express those feelings. She wanted to externalize her internal sense of obliteration.

This happens so often.

"We are destroyed, and then we seek to enact that destruction somewhere, to give it form," I said. "And that destruction can come out against self or other."

By her face, I could see that this hit home.

"So what do I do?" she asked.

"Can you surrender to the feelings, can you stay conscious through the destruction without unconsciously acting them out against yourself?"

Lisa is a gutsy and intense woman, not inclined to shrink back from challenge—or truth.

She recognized the irony: Lisa the warrior would surrender so that Lisa the warrior could continue to be.

30

Duration of Grief

I have faith in nights.
—RAINER MARIA RILKE

I'M OFTEN ASKED the question about grief's duration.

Just this morning I had an email from a sibling grieving a murdered brother who asked, "How long will this take?"

The people who ask me such things are often the newly bereaved or those who deeply care for them, wishing for life to be as it once was. For those grieving, it is impossible to imagine that this peculiar and idiosyncratic pain will ever end, that life will ever be "normal" again, that the tears will run dry.

And truly, things cannot and will not ever be exactly as they were—because we and our world are changed.

Some claim that it is time that heals, but I see this process a bit differently.

Certainly, time allows some necessary space, a kind of respite, from the despair of early grief. Personally, though, I don't actually feel that my grief has diminished over time.

I can still access the deep, vivid grief of losing Cheyenne.

The idea that grief incrementally weakens by the mere passage of time has not been my truth.

Nor would I wish it to be.

It isn't how much time has passed that counts. It's what we—and others around us—do with that time.

I DECIDED EARLY that I would not be willing to fragment parts of myself in order to make me—or those around me—comfortable. And, by allowing myself to be with grief, to bear its weight, to carry it, I have become stronger.

Eventually I became strong enough to help others carry their grief.

If we were to use a 1–10 scale, my grief varies day to day across the whole range, but my capacity to cope is almost always (in recent years) at a 9 or a 10.

It happened like this:

Slowly at first, very slowly, I started to stretch and exercise my "grief-bearing muscles" by being with my pain. Carrying such formidable weight, my muscles hurt at first—almost constantly, they ached and burned with pain—as my body objected to the new weight I had to carry.

Over time, as I kept stretching, kept lifting grief's weight, I grew stronger and more flexible—becoming better able to carry grief in all its myriad shape-shifting forms. The weight I needed to bear never changed—only my ability to carry it.

I wanted to adapt to the weight rather than having to overcome it, to force healing, or to be at war with my grief or myself.

And through such adaption, my heart has grown bigger, and my capacity to learn from and transform suffering has also enlarged.

Even so, I would gladly give back my newfound strength and flexibility to have Cheyenne. And yet, the other side of that truth is that decades later I am more whole today than I would have been without having known and loved my daughter.

THOSE WE LOVE DEEPLY who have died are part of our identity; they are a part of our biography.

We feel that love in the marrow of our bones.

There is a lingering call to remember them that, though sometimes muted by the chaos of the world, never fades away. When we dismiss that call, the cost to ourselves is fragmentation and disconnection, and the cost to society is an emotional impoverishment that ignores grief and causes it to be reborn into self-and-other. Seeking to live without grief, we diminish our ability to feel truly content.

Turning toward the shattered pieces of our selves, choosing to stand in the pain, is a serious responsibility. When we remember our beloved dead, we bridge the gap of space and time between us and them and bring them back into the whole of our reality.

Particularly when life has regained a tempo of comfort, surrendering to grief is an act of necessary courage.

31

The Courage to Remember

Once you have faced the Great Death,
the second death can do you no harm.

—FRANCIS OF ASSISI

LARRY WAS A MIDDLE-AGED MAN whose mother was from the Diné tribe and whose father was the son of an Irish immigrant. Sadness was etched in the wrinkles on his leathery face and deepened when he described, with surprising ease, a panoply of physical ailments. Larry was referred to me by a psychiatrist who felt that many of the physiological symptoms Larry was experiencing were related to protracted grief. His son, Matthew, was almost ten years old when he died of leukemia—more than twenty-five years ago.

Larry described how he did "really well" coping with Matthew's death for the first few months. He and his then-wife felt closer having shared such a traumatic loss. Larry was focused on helping her and their younger son cope with the "one thing that changed it all."

About six months after Matthew's death, Larry began feeling angry, and its expression felt uncontrollable to him: he would launch into rages, breaking furniture and throwing dishes. While he never physically harmed his family, he knew these behaviors were problematic. Over the next few months, Larry felt his wife and son slipping away from him, and so he left. He had lived in nine states over twenty-three years, changing jobs frequently, and felt inconsolable guilt and shame for having abandoned his wife and only living child.

He had not visited Matthew's gravesite since leaving home.

During our early days together, Larry didn't share too much

emotional content; he focused a great deal on those outward expressions of inner feelings that had so harmed his relationship with his family.

Once I sensed that Larry trusted our relationship, I asked him to describe the time period when he felt he had coped "really well" with grief.

He said that he and his wife would visit Matthew's grave and decorate it.

They went on walks and remembered him.

They cried together.

On one visit to their home, however, Larry's parents encouraged him to "stop grieving" for "the sake of his family." They suggested that Matthew's photographs would be better put away in the family trunk. Their family admonished Larry and his wife for being too consumed with their grief. Larry's work, too, pushed him forward before he was ready: they discouraged him from talking about Matthew at work because it might upset his colleagues. From all sides, Larry was getting a message to disavow grief and thus, in a sense, to forget the love he continued to feel for Matthew.

"What if they were all wrong?" I asked him after one particularly painful meeting. "What if you never needed to forget the grief you felt in order to be a good husband and father? What if that grief would have, instead, served a purpose of enacting love for him?"

It was the first time in months of meeting together that Larry would weep.

We had begun the arduous process of grieving and re-grieving for Matthew.

This meant many things for Larry: writing letters, looking at photographs, telling the story again in a different context, connecting with his deep pain, guilt, and shame. It meant visiting Matthew's grave. It meant finding his ex-wife and his living son and asking their forgiveness.

He did reconnect with his living son, and their relationship began to strengthen and grow.

About two years into our work together, Larry moved to be near him.

WHILE LARRY'S SYMPTOMS PERSISTED—many them perhaps simply functions of aging—his deep psychological pain had been brought out into his conscious awareness, and so he understood himself better and he felt more connected to himself, to Matthew, and to his life. Larry began socializing with others, building friendships, and even dating—something he hadn't done for many years.

An important part of this process was to tell others with whom he felt connected that he had *two* children, one living and one who had died.

And Larry felt Matthew's presence more often, an aspect of his journey that would be crucial to his own healing.

Last I heard from Larry was on the anniversary of Matthew's death. He visited the gravesite and sent me a photo. He had left a baseball cap from Matthew's favorite team on his grave.

And he thanked me for helping him find the courage to remember his son, as an essential element in becoming fully human.

32

Joining Hands

Let's stop making deals for a safe passage.
—JOYCE WELLWOOD

MANY PEOPLE ASK OF THOSE GRIEVING: "Are you still feeling so sad?" "How long will you be feeling so sad?" "What can we do to stop you from feeling so sad?"

The thing about grief is that there isn't a place or time at which we arrive once-and-for-all at peace, or healing, or completion.

Grief is a process, an unending long and winding road. The landscape changes as we travel the distance, some parts of the path barren and some more beautiful—but it's the same road. And grief itself is the destination: at every moment of our grief, we are arriving.

But so many of us receive the antithetical message from within medical, spiritual, educational, and social systems that grief is pathological, a condition to be treated, cured, and eradicated. These messages from a compassion-deficient culture, explicit or tacitly embedded into the appraisal of normative grief, inform and influence our relationship to bereavement. This is one of the greatest challenges to the bereaved.

Our culture is rife with platitudes, psychologically imperialistic idioms, that propagate its understanding of grief. Some of these will sound familiar to any griever:

- "S/he is in a better place."
- "S/he isn't suffering anymore."

- "Everything happens for a reason."
- "It's time to move on, to move forward."
- "It's not normal to feel that way."
- "Grieving can easily become a mental disorder."
- "Your *(child, spouse, parent, grandchild, etc.)* wouldn't want you to be sad."
- "I can't believe you are *still* feeling grief."
- "Maybe you should get on some medication."
- "Shouldn't you feel better by now?"
- "It's not normal to hurt for this long."
- "You can have *other* children."
- "You have to forget this."
- "Trust in God's plan."
- "Just let go."
- "God needed an angel to tend His garden."
- "Try *(this therapy, that technique)* to help you heal."
- "Don't think about it."
- "Just think happy thoughts."
- "Try to remember the good times."
- "Don't think about the bad times."
- "Just replace the hard memories with good ones."
- "You have to get back to life."

Other members of grief-denying culture, fearful that the emotional contagion of grief will expose them to their own pain, try to justify their avoidance and defend themselves from the unthinkable. They try to *fix* grief—my friend the renowned psychotherapist Dr. Robert Stolorow calls this "the War on Grief."

Other children or remarriage will not cure this.

It *is* normal to feel this way and for this long.

And there is no "better place" for those we love than with us.

Grief cannot, and should not, be fixed.

Our culture is terrified by powerful expression of painful emotions and so uses its institutions and agencies to quell grief, to force people into dark corners of hiding, to silence grieving wails with pills, to forcibly calm and control that which should not be controlled. It uses its platitudes to perpetuate myths and misinformation about what is normal in grieving, and the temptation to move away from our own suffering is real and seemingly sensible to some.

Yet there is no place for the tidy, the neat, or the civilized in mourning.

Grief violates convention: it is raw, primal, seditious, chaotic, writhing, and most certainly uncivilized. Yet grief is an affirmation of human passion, and only those who are apathetic, who stonewall love, who eschew intimacy can escape grief's pull.

No intervention and no interventionist can "cure" our grief. And we are not broken—we are brokenhearted.

Grief is not a medical disorder to be cured.

Grief is not spiritual crisis to be resolved.

Grief is not a social woe to be addressed.

Grief is, simply, a matter of the heart—to be felt.

As the Kotzker Rebbe, a nineteenth-century Hasidic rabbi, said: "There is no heart more whole than a broken one."

33

The Power of Unprocessed Traumatic Grief

Though we encounter it as suffering,
grief is in fact an affirmation.

—LEON WIESELTIER

WHEN I FIRST MET GRETCHEN, she shared her intense fear that her mother, Jade, was going to die of alcoholism and other substance abuse, both prescription and street.

Gretchen was a young, single woman who had spent much of her life parentified: she and her mother had reversed roles. Gretchen became the caregiver and Jade the self-destructive youth. Gretchen vacillated between taking care of Jade and withdrawing from her.

Jade had been sexually abused as a child and experienced the deaths of many people close to her, including her own mother and her husband, Gretchen's father, who had died painfully of cancer when Gretchen was a teenager. Jade had mastered fragmentation, assisted by the revolving door of substance abuse and treatment centers— which addressed the alcohol abuse with psychiatric medications. Jade would abuse those too and add more alcohol—increasing doses of both—in a continuous attempt to numb her emotional pain. Medical structures, in focusing only on Jade's damaging management of distress but failing to address historical grief and trauma, had not provided the much-needed compassionate support and psychoeducation. This perpetuated the vicious cycle of self-injury that widened the gap between Jade and her support system.

Gretchen was the only person who wouldn't give up on Jade,

repeatedly sacrificing her own emotional, financial, and social stability trying to reach her mother.

For about a year and a half, Jade titrated off all her medications and claimed sobriety. She was in counseling, though that counseling did not address her traumatic grief. Nonetheless, for a while, Jade abstained from substances and was coping with many of the superficial problems that had accumulated from years of self-medication, but she had not yet come face-to-face again with the nucleus of her traumatic grief. And so, without the adequate infrastructure of a trauma-informed therapist, she would slip back into the hole of despair, desperately trying to claw her way out using the only means she knew from her past: self-medication.

One horrible summer day about a year later, Gretchen would go to check on Jade because she hadn't answered her phone calls.

She found Jade dead in her house.

Gretchen felt groundless, homeless, and filled with guilt and shame over her mother's death: "I dismissed my mother's grief. I got tired of hearing it. . . . All she wanted was to be heard, seen, loved. I didn't listen, couldn't see her, and loved her from a distance. I live with that and hope to one day not feel such responsibility for her life and the part I feel I played in her death."

In her own grief work, through being with painful emotions, Gretchen expressed her heart's inscape with this verse:

Mother, daughter / Pure love / You were my best friend growing
    up / You were my mom / Alcohol became your need / Alcohol
    became my hate / Alcohol took you away / When did we
    switch roles? / When did I become the mother?
You drank / I'd worry / You drank / I'd cry / Hope crushed by
    each drink you took / Years went by / Fear grew strong that
    you were going to die /
Sobriety came / You stopped drinking / We switched roles / You
    mother, me daughter / Relief Joy Pride / A year and a half you

were my mom / A year and a half I was your daughter / That
first drink crushed me / You were dying right before my eyes
/ You stopped calling / You didn't answer your phone / Fear
rushed through me / She's dead / No, just drunk / Months go
by / Drinking takes over your soul / The demons were winning
No, no, no this can't be happening / Tears fall / Body trembles /
Mind is frozen / Grieving you / Missing you / Suddenly a little
girl needing her momma / I yearn for you / I cry for you / Did you
know my love? / I feel lost without you / Regret / Guilt / Pain
How could I walk away? / How could I not see you? / You're
dead / You're missed / You're loved / You're my mom / I'm
your daughter / I'm sorry, I'm sorry, I'm sorry / You deserved
more / Alcohol blinded us both / Alcohol destroyed us both
I miss you / I love you
You're my momma / I'm your daughter

THE STORY OF GRETCHEN AND JADE illuminates the process by which a
broken system adds suffering to those who suffer, and this is one way
in which traumatic grief is transmitted intergenerationally.

Gretchen is now fraught with her own suffering because of Jade's
death, which itself had been hastened through avoidance of Jade's
own traumatic grief.

And this entire cycle was worsened by a system that failed to provide the kind of compassionate care that might have redirected a fatal
trajectory.

Those who misappropriate authority over grief can do lasting
damage.

34

Silenced for Decades

> What restraint or limit should there be
> to grief for one so dear?
> —HORACE

IN A SINGLE DAY RECENTLY, I received four emails from grievers around the world who have been harmed by ill-advised interventions aiming to *fix* grief.

From one grieving mom: "I started to cry and my therapist interrupted me and said there was no need to cry. She told me to start tapping on my face instead. I felt such shame for my tears."

From another: "He said it had been too long and that because I still cried every day I should go to an inpatient unit for psychiatric disorders. I was tortured while I was there—nothing short of torture. I was strapped down when I didn't want to take the medications. It was horror."

And from a grieving husband: "The pastor told me that God didn't want me to be sad anymore. And so the only way around my sadness was to drink."

And yet another grieving mom shared how she is consistently met by coworkers who castigate her for keeping a photo of her child who died on her desk—because after four months it makes them uncomfortable and because she "needs to move on." (I invited this mom to consider the possibility that it is their fear, not her inadequacy or inappropriateness, that is at issue here.)

On another day in March of 2013, I received a letter from Anne, an elderly woman whose grief went unseen by others:

Dear Dr. Joanne,

I cannot express just what your work means to me. You see, I lost my baby, Barbara on February 15th, 1966. Barbara lived just 16 hours—she was full-term, actually 11 days overdue. I was in the hospital, in labor for 37½ hours. I know they should have done a C-section, but I was a clinic patient and was told all 5 doctors had to agree and they could not get all 5 together. My husband and I were young, knew no better, and in those days, more than trusted a doctor's word. There were no bereavement groups. I had asked for a priest, as this was a Catholic hospital, yet no one ever came to try to help me through this horror. When communion was distributed, we had to go into the hallway.

I was so torn from the stitches of a breech birth, could barely walk also from the weakness. I went into deep, deep inconsolable grief, and I was so lonely. No one would talk about her. I had another child, almost 3, to take care of and hold and love, but it did not help my loneliness.

By September, my husband finally took me to the doctor, who put me on antidepressants that made my body feel so heavy, I could barely lift my head, much less take care of my little girl. And she herself was going through a terrible time as she was told she had a baby sister, and then had to be told the baby was ill, could not come home, and finally that she went to heaven. No three-year-old could comprehend this.

I have never gotten over my loss, even all these years later. My arms still feel so empty, and I never got to see Barbara. In my mind, I picture her either in the room with tubes and machines or in a tiny white casket, dressed in her christening outfit that my brother bought for her.

When I heard you say that babies' lives matter, and that my grief is real and valid and that someone should have helped me back then, I cried—as I knew I'd found the place to talk, and hopefully, begin to heal. You see Dr. Joanne, back then, I did not fit into "loss of child" because others didn't see her death as a real loss. But to me, she is more real than anything and so is my love for her.

I want to thank you for creating and sharing your work. I lost my husband 5½ years ago to cancer with many terrible complications. It took me awhile, but found I could help others through becoming a hospice volunteer, even though we did not have hospice. It was my way or making his and Barbara's lives have meaning.

Again, I thank you for your work, for your words, and for helping me.

Maybe now, I can heal.

God Bless You!

Anne

For nearly five decades, Anne's suffering was shrouded in silence.

Some of the suffering was worthy and necessary: the grief of losing her second child, Barbara, and what that would do to the entire family system.

Much of the suffering, though, was unnecessary: the kind of suffering created by her experience with people who passively acquiesced to a system that promulgated evasion and fear instead of approaching and love.

Grief demands to be seen and felt—and when we see it and feel it, grief will break our hearts open into sweeping expansion.

Anne, after forty-seven years, was finally able to come back to herself—restored to her basic human right to grieve—but she needed others, as do we all, to help carry the burden of surrender.

We need others to remember with us.

We need compassion.

We need empathy.

We need to find within us the courage to slowly stretch and strengthen our grief-bearing muscles so that one day, we are better able to cope with grief's weight and, perhaps, one day, to help another.

BE SKEPTICAL OF THE ADVICE YOU INTERNALIZE.

Find those who are willing to join you and walk with you nonjudgmentally.

Steer clear of those who claim to have a cure for your grief.

Surround yourself instead with those who admit they have no answers but who will enter into the realm of unknowing with you.

Seek others doing real soul work and join hands with them, your tribe.

Listen deeply and you will recognize other citizens of the country of sorrow.

They are many, and they are beautiful.

35

Guilt and Shame

The pain is there; when you close one door on it,
it knocks to come in somewhere else.

—IRVIN D. YALOM

THE WORD *surrender* means to give back something or yield ourselves over to something. In the context of grieving, we give ourselves over to grief.

Anything that takes us from our routine of life into the sacred space of intentional grief can be part of a surrendering practice. This may mean revisiting a support group; it may mean retelling our story again and again, focusing on the associated feelings rather than facts during each narration; and it may mean writing out our story of love and grief every few months or years—and seeing how it may start to change or grow.

The inner perspective seeks birthing—it must be outwardly borne and witnessed—and the outer perspective seeks to be internalized and integrated.

In my own case, while some details of Cheyenne's death in 1994 remain constant, the qualitative aspects of her death have shifted dramatically for me. Intentionally revisiting my own story of loss is one way I give myself back, surrendering, to each revision.

Finding specific words for our present-moment experiences of the loss can also be helpful.

GLENN, a man who had lost his thirty-seven-year-old wife, Julie, to a motor vehicle accident, had difficulty expressing his feelings. He frequently used the same four adjectives to describe how he felt: *sad, angry, confused*, and *lost*. It had been about two years since Julie's death when we started meeting.

He said he was growing weary of hearing his story, hearing it sounding the same—over and over. So I invited him to carefully consider the words he chose to describe his feelings. Glenn would take one night a week to find more specific words better suited to the particular emotion arising in the moment.

One week, *anger* became "fire in the pit of my belly" and *sadness* became "feeling as if someone reached into my chest and pulled out my heart." As we began to work with the specific feelings, as Glenn began to give himself over to each unfolding moment, he noticed the capaciousness of his emotions.

He began to tell the story of "date night" with Julie and—while he often cried—he also started to realize a bottomless depth of gratitude for their time together, even though far too limited. Glenn had previously believed any "good" feelings that might arise were a betrayal of Julie. Yet through keeping the "adjective journal," he realized that, rather than being mutually exclusive, the "good" feelings coexisted with the painful ones. His feelings seemed to flow more with this practice—even the feelings of guilt for having survived her, which were there whether or not he was awake to them.

Many bereaved people struggle with issues of guilt and shame. This is particularly true in cases of traumatic grief and, especially, when a child dies or when one person is directly responsible for another person's death.

Just the process of staying present with shame and guilt in a safe space can help to neutralize those emotions' potency. In such a place, we can abandon the need to judge feelings as *right* or *wrong* or *good* or *bad*.

This alone has the power to diffuse and dilute them.

ALEXANDRA WAS RESPONSIBLE for the death of her only child, Maggie. I met her two years after Maggie's death.

She had become a master of disguise, always pretending to be happy—which meant not remembering Maggie. She had become a kind of "avoidance ninja." It's easy to see why she felt she had to: Maggie had died as a result of head trauma after Alexandra had lost hold of a television she had been trying to move. Alexandra hadn't realized that Maggie was in the room with her.

Our work together began when Alexandra realized she'd been drinking too much and needed help. She would frequently lament the role she had played in her child's death, and yet, when she would speak with others about her feelings, they dismissed her guilt, urging her to forgive herself or not to think about it.

They denied what Alexandra knew to be a core truth: though not intentional, Alexandra's actions had indeed caused Maggie's death, and Alexandra needed a safe place to talk about her guilt and shame.

Since she could not find that safe place, she stopped talking about it altogether. She grew weary of the knee-jerk reactions she got from others: "Don't blame yourself" or "You shouldn't feel guilty" or "She wouldn't want you to be sad" or "Don't cry, it'll be okay." While these messages came to her under the guise of sympathy, to Alexandra they felt dishonest, coercive, and self-serving. She felt invalidated rather than seen. What she longed for was a refuge for her darkest moments, a witness for the most agonizing aspects of grief, which were still pleading for a safe place to be seen.

She told me that she didn't want someone to help her feel less guilty.

She didn't want someone to help her feel less despair.

She didn't want someone to help her find happiness.

And this was a good fit for the kind of work I do. I don't help people feel good. I help people *feel*: without judgment, without trying to change anything, without averting my gaze. We would spend many hours together with her shame and guilt, both of which we consciously welcomed during our work together. Such guests needed to be given a place to be accepted, and I sensed Alexandra's need for some expression or expiation. She was now able to share those feelings safely—and in so doing she sought atonement and a way to speak of her contrition to Maggie.

IT WAS FIFTEEN YEARS EARLIER when my own sense of failure—my own guilt and shame—sent me seeking absolution. My daughter had been dead for more than a year. In a desperate moment, I sat on the floor with a black wire-bound notebook and began writing to her: *Dear Cheyenne*, I started, as tears flowed. I put the notebook down and lay limply on the carpet. I started again. *Dear Cheyenne, I am so sorry, baby. I am so, so, so sorry.* I would go on to write four pages of *I'm so sorry* followed by confessions of my wrongdoings—"wrong" thoughts (like "I should have known you were dying") and "wrong" feelings (like "I shouldn't be feeling these things"). I would end asking her forgiveness: *Please, baby, please, forgive me. I would give my life for you. Please, forgive me. I love you, I love you, I love you. I will always love you. I'm so sorry, so very sorry. Always.—Mommy.*

It took me quite a while to finish that letter—and it was excruciating.

I wept. I waited and read the letter again. I wept more. It had been awhile since I'd cried like that—a good marathon cry. It hurt, and it felt good.

Then I got still, pausing with heart turned inward, and waited. In the gap between breaths something very interesting happened.

I opened the notebook, grabbed the pen, and began free writing, writing rapidly and without thinking beforehand. What I wrote started like this: *Dear Mommy*—and then, in her little girl voice, Cheyenne wrote back to me her own affirmation of love, granting forgiveness even though I was not yet willing to forgive myself.

To say this was an extraordinary moment would not be enough.

It did not assuage my guilt and shame, but it shifted something in my mother's heart, maybe in my soul. It was a pivotal moment for me in my relationship to Cheyenne—and to my grief.

WHILE ALEXANDRA WAS NEVER ABLE to return the letter from Maggie to her, it was an important and emotional exercise: apologizing, asking forgiveness, and expressing an undying love that endures beyond this world.

36

Inward and Outward

Here we are all in one place,
The wants and wounds of the human race.
Despair and hope sit face to face
When you come in from the cold.
—CARRIE NEWCOMER

I MET MITCH two days after he backed a truck over his son.

He had been in a hurry to buy birthday supplies he'd forgotten for his older child's party, and he didn't notice that Lamar had followed him outside. Mitch's shock was palpable, and even now he still didn't really comprehend the full extent of this tragedy. At this early point, all I was able to do was provide a place of safety and to minimize added trauma.

Mitch was committed to his church and could not fathom that God could allow this to happen. His entire world felt like it was collapsing. And, in the center, there the fact was: he had caused this pain and agony for everyone; he was its source. It was too much to bear at that point. And Mitch dared not face other parents whose children had died; he dared not tell his story to strangers for fear of the gaze of accusation.

Though Mitch's wife was earnestly forgiving, every time she wept he was reminded how he "did this to her."

A few months later, Mitch would write a letter to Lamar.

He shared the letter with his wife and his parents.

He wanted to do this in my office.

I wept.

Everyone wept.

And then, opening his heart outward toward others, Mitch also shared the letter that Lamar had written back to him.

There was extraordinary pain and palpable love present in that room.

Later, Mitch told me he felt his intimacy with his wife and family had deepened noticeably.

Shortly after that, Mitch would resume church attendance for the first time since Lamar's death. And he also asked his pastor to speak with me about traumatic grief so the pastor would better know how to help Mitch and his family as the months and years passed.

IN BEING WITH GRIEF, our hearts are turned primarily inward with a focus on the self. In surrendering to grief, our focus vacillates between self and other. We learn to be with grief, even years later when it asks to be seen and felt, and as our own hearts soften and open, we also begin to more clearly see others' pain.

There are few places where this progression—turning inward, vacillating between inward and outward, and more clearly seeing others—is more noticeable than when I'm facilitating support group.

People often initially attend a group seeking another person whose story closely resembles their own. They want an image of self in some other. Even so, many experience a gradual softening of the heart toward those whose stories are different. And the ability to expand our sense of empathic connection grows.

MARGARET was a fiercely intelligent and fidgety middle-aged woman who wore oversize clothes and well-molded Birkenstocks even through winter. She attended her first support group only six weeks after her seventeen-year-old son's death by suicide. In the group, she met a couple whose son, age nineteen, had also died by suicide several years earlier. As that couple told their story, Margaret was captivated.

Her toes wiggled madly, up and down, as if every part of her recognized her own suffering in their words. They were the only other parents there that night who had faced the suicide of a child, and after the meeting, Margaret clung to them. For many months, she would share with me privately that she could not relate to the other parents whose children died of other causes and at different ages, and she distanced herself from them and limited her points of contact with them.

It was about nine months later when another mother shared with the group something about the death of her newborn. This mother reported feeling like an outcast, feeling disenfranchised. She talked about the ways in which others devalued her grief and her child because of when and how her daughter had died.

Margaret looked up at her—and began crying. I looked down at her toes, squirming and fidgety. Margaret recognized her story in this mother's very different narrative. As her heart opened and she found herself able to relate to more and more grieving parents, her circle of compassion grew, encompassing increasing numbers of suffering others. This surprised Margaret, and she felt especially vulnerable and strangely strong.

The paradox of suffering was becoming evident to her.

SIMILARLY, Andrea was a twenty-eight-year-old woman who had lost her father to suicide, and initially she related to people with very similar stories. Slowly over the next three years, her "circle of relatability" expanded to include children whose parents had died of other causes, and then grieving parents, grieving grandparents, and grieving spouses. The last time I saw Andrea, she was attending a general support group for all losses.

She felt a part of the group, and she often cried for others. And now Andrea is herself facilitating a grief group.

Andrea had learned to use her own broken heart, her own willingness to suffer, to expand the compassion she felt for others in what she called "a weird and wonderful and heartbreaking journey."

As we cultivate a practice of surrendering, of being with suffering, we will see that our own circle of relatability—that sense of oneness with the other—widens. Our own pain gives us access to an inexhaustible wellspring of compassion.

Ever so slowly, with compassionate support from others, unhurried time to mourn, self-care, and ritual, we can see that grief does something unusual.

Rather than abating or diminishing, it creates space, it moves over, it expands our heart's capacity to both sides of the paradox of pain and love—for ourselves and others.

We engage this process by feeling.

And remembering.

37

Works of Love

It is one's duty to love those we do not see.

—SØREN KIERKEGAARD

I'VE ALWAYS FOUND Kierkegaard's *Works of Love* comforting and validating.

In it, he says that remembering our dead epitomizes the most unselfish, freest, and most faithful type of love—a love willing to suffer for itself, so that it can continue to exist. It is unselfish because it is unrequited; our calling to our beloved dead cannot be reciprocated in the ways we so desire. It is freest because there is no coercion or obligation to continue loving the dead; it can only be an act of choice. It is faithful because it requires devotion; for neither affection, nor strength, nor kindness can be returned from one who has died.

Our dead do nothing to hold on to us; still, in remembering our dead, we love faithfully and with our unwavering intention. We hold open their place in our hearts.

With respect to one dead, Kierkegaard says,

> nothing is coercive at all. On the other hand, the loving memory of one dead has to protect itself against . . . new impressions to expel the memory, and it has to protect itself against time. . . . Time has a dangerous power; in time it is so easy to make a beginning again and thereby to forget. . . . In the meantime, the multiplicity of life's demands beckons to one; the living beckon to one and say: come to us, we will take care of you. One who is dead, however, cannot beckon.

And he offers us this advice:

> If you love one dead, then remember him lovingly . . . learn the kindness of thought, the definiteness in expression, the strength in unchangeableness, the pride in life which you would not be able to learn as well from any human being, even the most highly gifted. . . . Remember one who is dead, and in addition to the blessing which is inseparable from this work of love, you will also have the best guidance to understanding life: that it is one's duty to love those we do not see, but also those we do see.

MARIE'S SIX-MONTH-OLD BABY, Chance, died of SIDS. At first, Marie felt her grief deeply and openly expressed her sorrow. But over time, she was worn down by the familiar messages of our grief-denying culture. She felt as if she couldn't talk about Chance, not honestly anyway, and that openly expressing her grief was taboo. So she stopped talking about him, and she started to forget him, began to become unable to imagine his face.

Marie came to me almost ten years later, now anguishing over her loss. After we had committed to being with grief, revisiting the painful story she had rarely told, she asked me to help her create something to remember Chance.

We decided on a box that would hold all the memories others would share about him; we called it "Chance's Box." She emailed family and friends and asked them to write down memories of Chance, or of Marie being pregnant, or other related moments (such as, "Marie, I remember the day we heard you were pregnant" or "I remember the look on your face when you met Chance for the first time"). She then printed and laminated the stories into strips that would fit into Chance's Box. When Marie felt she was forgetting Chance, she'd dip into his box and pull out a random memory.

This practice was sustaining for Marie, and almost two decades later, she still uses his box on days when she longs to feel close to him.

MOST OFTEN, in very early grief, people say that one of their greatest fears is that others will forget. I, too, had that fear.

Initially, in the first few years after Cheyenne died, when my memories of her started to fade—which they did—when I would find it more difficult to recall her skin, her fingers, her smell, her essence, I panicked. So I wrote down every little detail and pulled out every photo. I held the memories to my heart. I said, "Please, please, don't forget, please." I *practiced* remembering her.

And so, even after all these years, I haven't forgotten.

I can still remember.

THE PLEA FOR CLOSENESS to our dead can always be heard—if we are still, if we listen.

When we ignore that call for too long, we fragment.

When we remember them, we bring the whole of their existence back into our hearts.

38

Waves of Grief

Between grief and nothing, I will take grief.
—WILLIAM FAULKNER

I MADE EFFORTS to remember Cheyenne, again and again. And even years after her death, remembering her comes with re-grieving. So I found myself, at times, resisting doing that work. I had many stories to justify that resistance: I was too busy. I had deadlines to meet. I had waves to catch with my surfboard.

ONE SUMMER, I was at Moonlight Beach surfing during a red tide. Despite warnings from more skilled surfers, I attempted to ride the waves, but the tide beat me—repeatedly, dangerously.

When I got back to the beach, I reflected on what surfing had taught me about grief.

There were times I felt like I was catapulted into the dark, deep water where waves of pain crashed down upon me relentlessly. Grief, like a powerful rip tide, pulled me into its black water and carried me, against my will, far from the familiar shore. I could no longer see my home, my life, or my self between the surges that hammered me. I fought for the slightest glimpse of sky.

The waves persisted.

They tumbled me, over and over and over, disorienting and confusing me. Deeper and deeper, the rip tide pulled me under water. I was gasping for air.

I fought the grief, but it was much stronger—I could not win.

Then grief whispered into my ear with a firm tenderness,

"Surrender—you won't die from the pain." And for a brief moment, I heeded. Surprised, I reached the surface for a desperate, pocket of air only to panic and resist again wrenching me back under the dark waters of grief that filled my lungs.

I knew I would not survive unless I surrendered.

And so I surrendered.

I relaxed into the tide, and it guided me to the surface, carrying me to shore—familiar, yet not—where it would release me.

Any surfer knows there is no other way to survive such a force of nature. The surfer's mantra is just this: surrender to the wave.

So, too, it is with waves of grief: surrender to the wave. I entrusted myself to both the calm and raging motions of grief. I was patient with its unpredictability, patient with the bitter taste it left in my mouth, and in exchange, it was kinder to me. We became cautious comrades—and I found my way back home.

This was how I survived in those early months and years of grief.

I stopped questioning myself—my emotions, my tears, my thoughts, my rituals, my suffering—and I let it all be. I surrendered.

I no longer punished myself for my failure to complete grieving within the allotted three-month period. I relinquished the rehearsed smile and perfunctory joy. I acknowledged my sadness whenever I felt it. I could be, simply and genuinely, me.

This is the gift of surrender: a deepened sense of authenticity and trust in myself.

EVEN THESE MANY YEARS LATER, I am occasionally overtaken by the rip tide—and the sea. I perform our dance many times, over and over again.

I remember her and re-grieve many times, over and over again.

For me it was the rip tide that dragged me under and took away my breath; for another grieving woman it was a different kind of darkening: "I would feel this shadow, terrifying, come down, and I felt I couldn't breathe. So I would push it away—never asking the shadow what it wanted. I didn't know it. It scared me—until I explored it and learned that it wasn't as scary as I'd thought. I began to talk to the shadow, and it talked to me. And I realized I could handle it."

When we are caught in a rip tide or overtaken by a shadow, we can trust that this moment will pass and we will regain the ability to breathe again—at least for a while.

39

"Remember Me," She Said

Love doesn't die,
People do.
—MERRIT MALLOY

IN EARLY SPRING OF 2000, I was planning for an annual retreat for bereaved parents. I'd wanted to dedicate the conference to the work of Dr. Elisabeth Kübler-Ross, a woman whose words influenced me in the early days of my grief. I went looking for photographs of her to use in our program. I found one I liked: Elisabeth amid a field of daisies.

I'd only had one dream of Cheyenne at this point, and it was of her running through a field of daisies and holding on to an oversize straw hat. I ran behind trying to catch her.

I emailed the photographer to ask his permission to use it. The next day, he wrote back asking what its use would be. I explained.

After several more emails back and forth—telling him about Chey's death, why I wanted this photo, and how Dr. Kübler-Ross had influenced my early grief journey—he said, "I think you should call her. Here's her number. My mom would love to meet you."

I was stunned! His *mom*?

I think I emailed him back and told him I was too scared to call. But eventually I did. It turned out she lived just a few miles from me. And so, the next day, I was headed to the home of Dr. Elisabeth Kübler-Ross—with a plate of her favorite angel hair pasta marinara.

I visited Elisabeth often, sometimes three or four days a week, for the rest of her life.

We would watch movies together, eat popcorn, and talk about grief and death.

During the course of our friendship, I occasionally wanted to give up my work with traumatic grief, disheartened by the never-ending sadness of child death.

Elisabeth gently reminded me that *I* hadn't chosen this course in the first place.

"Continue, Joanne," she added. "You have to continue."

EXACTLY ONE MONTH before her death, I had a dream that Elisabeth died.

In my dream, I was sobbing—desperate to have my friend back.

When I visited Elisabeth the next day, I told her that I had dreamed about her the previous night.

"Was it a good dream?" she asked.

"Well, not really."

"Did I die?"

"Yes."

"Well, then that was a good dream," she said—with an impish smile.

Elisabeth told me that she was eager to die, and I actually knew that to be true. And she told me that whenever I remembered her, she would be right there, with me. And yet I walked away from our conversation knowing it would be very hard for me to say goodbye.

I CAME HOME the night of Elisabeth's funeral services exhausted and aching—already missing her so much and feeling grief's grip around my chest. The grief felt cumulative. It was grief for losing her. Grief for losing my mom only three years earlier. And of course, grief over losing Cheyenne.

Around 11 p.m., I went onto my front patio and sat in my rocking chair, thinking of Elisabeth and talking to her in my mind. I asked her for a clear sign that what she had told me was true: that if I remembered her, she'd be with me. I closed my eyes.

I knew it was silly.

Even so, a few minutes later, when I opened my eyes to the night sky, I saw a shooting star. Seeing it, I again heard her words in my head: *Remember me*.

I do know how to remember, I know how to call back those I love into my heart—even when those memories come with deep longing and sadness.

I remember Elisabeth—and she is with me.

40

Ritual and Microritual

Ritual is the antidote to helplessness.

—SUKIE MILLER

ONE ARIZONA SUMMER DAY, a young boy named Gurraj, five years old, was swimming with his younger brother and his parents. He suffered a seizure and died.

His parents, Gurvinder and Raj, called me only two hours after leaving the hospital.

I MET WITH THEM at their home, where Gurraj and his brother had played and where Gurvinder and Raj dreamed of their future as a family.

The family, surrounded by their Sikh community, was trying to understand their traumatic grief, feeling lost and overwhelmed. Pictures of Gurraj were all over, a beamingly happy boy with penetrating dark eyes. In one, I could see the *kara* he was wearing, the steel bracelet that symbolized beginninglessness and endlessness, God's eternal nature. In one room, family members took turns, they told me, in an uninterrupted reading aloud of the entire *Sri Guru Granth Sahib*, the Sikh holy book.

Gurraj's parents requested that I attend the Antam Sanskar, the funeral rites, and I felt tragically privileged to accompany them on the long road to farewell. They unfolded his thick hair, unshorn all five years of life, and told me this symbolized respect for the perfection of God's creation. They washed his entire body, weeping with grief. The elders of the community contributed their own wails of sorrow as they encircled Gurraj.

When the day of cremation arrived, hundreds of Sikhs came to say farewell. Gurvinder led the procession to the crematorium where, as is customary for the father of a child who dies, Raj lit the funeral pyre.

The rest of us stood by Gurvinder and wept.

RITUAL SERVES TO HONOR the contents of our hearts, both the love and pain. Every society has rituals associated with death and grief. They serve the function of *connection maintenance*—helping us feel closer to our loved one who has died. Emotional expression revives a sense of control, helps us feel meaning, and underpins communal structures within which we are better able to cope with our losses.

In the early days after loss, ritual tends toward being more public—with friends and family heavily involved, remembering and grieving with us. Such rituals may include candle-lighting vigils or remembrance services, sending cards and casseroles, planting a tree or making a donation in the name of the one who has died, sitting shiva, or holding a wake. Such shared rituals as these tend to happen at the beginning of grief and taper off as time passes. People go back to their lives, special community or family rituals wane, and such rituals as remain become increasingly more private, enacted in what I call *microrituals*.

There are microrituals in early grief too: holding, seeing, washing the dead, for instance. Later mircrorituals take other forms: large and well-planned (organizing a barefoot walk, a toy drive, or a musical activity) or spontaneous and small (such as saying "good morning" to the one who has died, burning incense, or praying and meditating). Microrituals can include attention to items of remembrance such as a phone bill, a favorite lipstick, handwritten notes, and other personal items. They can also include sacrificing something we value or want, from social engagement to physical comfort. And microrituals can go on for decades—indefinitely even.

Ritual acts, whether public or private, large-scale or small, are a means to unmask feelings of love and pain.

Microrituals are a purposeful means of invoking our beloved dead's presence in our day-to-day lives. One man, for example, says "Good morning, Pops" every single morning to his father who died. One woman hugs her husband's favorite shirt in the bed they shared for more than fifteen years. Another woman burns incense for her daughter who died at birth. A bereaved father lights a candle every night at dinner to honor his son who died in military combat.

These tiny acts carve out spaces in regular life specifically for touching our loved ones who've died.

I HAVE MANY of my own microritual practices.

For instance, in lieu of a New Year's resolution, I honor Cheyenne by composing an intention for the coming year. Here is one:

I intend to breathe my way through conflict,

To breathe my way through the great risks,

To breathe my way through the ebb and flow of grief,

To breathe my way through the muck and mire of life,

To breathe my way through dark disappointments.

I intend to be with my true self,

To listen for what is beneath the stillness,

To see the lingering pain of others,

To bow before the great teachers—children and nature,

To love all things more fully.

I intend to open my arms and my heart to the world,

remembering that we belong to each other.

Another microritual I employ is a sacrifice of speech with a "vow of silence day." I pin a little round piece of paper to my shirt that says, "Vow of Silence Day in honor of Cheyenne." This particular microritual is powerful for me, of course, and there is also something moving when another person realizes you've committed to a day of silence to remember one who has died. In a similar vein, every few months I take a vow of hunger, sacrificing food for a day to acknowledge hunger and poverty around the world.

Physical and emotional sacrifice is often a component of microrituals.

ON THE MORNING OF OCTOBER 18, 2010, five-year-old Jada sprawled herself across her sleeping mother, Zoey—waking her by saying, "Mama, I love you as pretty as a magnolia."

Jada and her brother Jordan were murdered that day.

Over the course of my work with Zoey—a period of years—she repeatedly used the microritual of tattooing, which became one way she could make outwardly apparent both her grief and her continuing love.

Her first tattoo would come six weeks after their deaths: Jada and Jordan's ashes tattooed into the back of her neck as an eternity symbol. Jada's words that day—"Mama, I love you pretty as a magnolia."—became another tattoo, another microritual of remembrance.

As did a line of verse from Robert Green Ingersoll: "In the night of death, hope sees a star, and listening love can hear the rustle of a wing." She had this tattooed alongside both of her children's names—and two lavender magnolias.

Zoey would often listen to one of Jordan's favorite pieces of music, "Soon We'll Be Found," by the singer Sia. She took solace in the song's lyrics: "So come along, it won't be long 'til we return happy. / Shut your eyes, there are no lies in this world we call sleep. / Let's desert this day of hurt, tomorrow we'll be free. / Turn around, I know we're lost but soon we'll be found."

She had the title of the song tattooed on her right rib cage to honor the fact that she and her children would find their way back to each other.

THROUGH ART AND CEREMONY, through narrative and creation, through act and speech and silence, through symbols and withstanding pain, rituals and microrituals help us remember.

And in that way, they help us to love.

41

Meaning through Compassionate Action

> Nothing can make up for the absence of someone we love,
> and it would be wrong to try and find a substitute; we must
> simply hold out and see it through. That sounds very hard
> at first, but at the same time it is a great consolation.
> It remains unfilled, preserves the bonds between us.
> —DIETRICH BONHOEFFER

COMPASSION IS MORE THAN JUST A FEELING.

Sometimes compassion means taking action, making connections. And it is precisely our own grief, our own pain, that enables us to connect to the suffering of others.

Beyond merely being with grief, we must also *do with* it.

In doing with grief, grief is not gone, or forgotten, or recovered from. Grief remains our partner, our companion—the source of our compassionate action in the world. When we *do with* grief, grief is being lived openly, honestly, ennoblingly.

Doing with grief can give life new meaning, even if this new meaning is unwanted and the sacrifice demanded far too great. Compassion arises when we yield to our own pain instead of evading it, when we allow our hearts to remain open and gracious.

And yet no part of the grief journey can ever be rushed—including meaning-seeking and compassionate action. Even these can be subverted into a bypass to hasten and move away from grief.

The redemptive potential of fully inhabited grief actualizes when our deepening self-awareness merges with our broadening other-awareness and swallows, in oneness, the space between. This synthesis of inward and outward, self and other, expresses the relationship we have with our loved ones who died. We meet them inside our hearts, and then we find ways to carry spirit into the world.

Suffering endured becomes compassion expressed.

Grieving becomes giving.

ONE DAY, while waiting for my acupuncture appointment, I noticed a quote on the wall: "My barn, having burned to the ground—I now see the moon." My first impulse was to tear it down; my second impulse was to throw myself into the chair and sob.

But I sat with it, for quite a while.

Decades after losing my daughter Cheyenne, this is indeed what it feels like for me.

Pain becomes wisdom.

We cannot help another without also helping ourselves.

42

Kindness Projects

Our loss, our wound, is precious to us because it can
wake us up to love, and to loving action.

—NORMAN FISCHER

IT WAS DECEMBER 24—a long five months since Cheyenne's death—
and I had mustered the courage to walk through the aisles of Toys
"R" Us, snotty tissues in my coat pockets, buying random toys for
random children, dimly imagined. Walking up and down the aisles,
surrounded by babies and young children, my body was seized with
emotional pain, and I want to sprint, wailing, from the store. But I
didn't. I took my finds to the checkout and paid for them.

Later that day, I wrapped each gift, carefully, and placed them in
a large, white garbage bag—like the kind I used to collect the dead
leaves fallen from the cottonwood tree—and, again, I wept.

This is not how I planned it to be.

It's not what I wanted.

My world, shattering over and over every single second, seemed
unbearable.

I didn't have a plan for distributing the toys. I only knew that from
being with my pain, I would also be with my love for her.

So I packed up my car and headed out, getting onto the freeway.
I'd intended to go to the children's hospital but ended up at a local
Head Start program. I didn't actually want to see the children, so I
gave my garbage bag of gifts to the center's director.

She thanked me.

I didn't want to be thanked.

I didn't want to be recognized.

If I could have just deposited the toys outside the front door, that would have felt better to me.

Still, I allowed her expression of gratitude to wash over me. It turned out, the director told me, there were six boys and eight girls that day in the center.

I went to my car and didn't start it. I just sat there and wept.

THAT CHRISTMAS EVE experience had such a great impact on me that I started doing more things, always anonymously and each time remembering Cheyenne.

One day I was at a shoe store, and I overheard two parents talking about which one of their four or five children was going to get new shoes. They were back-to-school shopping, and while they all needed shoes, the family could only afford one pair.

I thought of Cheyenne, and how we might have been shopping together that day.

Stealthily, I found the store manager and gave him enough money to ensure all those children would get new shoes. If there was a balance on the gift card, I asked that he give the balance to the parents. I wrote Cheyenne's name on a little piece of paper and handed it to him along with the money—and left.

In bringing Cheyenne into that present moment, in the space between my suffering and that family's pain, her love was alive in the world.

I kept doing these things.

Each time I engaged in a random act of generosity, and I noticed how healing it was for me.

This was the birth of the Kindness Project.

THE KINDNESS PROJECT had become a hallmark of the MISS Foundation.

We printed a thousand cards that said this:

THIS RANDOM ACT OF KINDNESS IS DONE IN LOVING MEMORY
OF OUR BEAUTIFUL CHILD.

That first thousand were gone within a week.

We printed more cards, in different languages.

We printed cards for other relationships from bereaved siblings, spouses, and grandparents to aunts, uncles, and friends. Those cards looked like this:

THIS RANDOM ACT OF KINDNESS IS DONE IN LOVING MEMORY OF

_____

WORD OF THE KINDNESS PROJECT spread through the bereaved community.

On July 27, 2011—the day we would declare International Kindness Project Day—more than 10,000 people around the world united to make use of free Kindness Project cards to engage in random acts of anonymous kindness in memory of a loved one who had died.

Since then, more than 2,000,000 acts of kindness have occurred globally in the United States and abroad—in Romania, Australia, Paraguay, Bermuda, the Netherlands, Spain, Mexico, New Zealand, Chile, Italy, Malta, and more—through the Kindness Project.

One couple anonymously paid for meals at restaurants in memory of their son.

A woman randomly wrapped a twenty-dollar bill around a Kindness Card and left it for a stranger to find.

Another made handmade dresses to ship to Haitian children in memory of her daughter who'd died twenty-four years earlier.

A couple paid for the adoption of sixteen dogs in memory of their sixteen-year-old son and left seventeen potted flowers next to random cars in memory of their seventeen-year-old daughter.

One person went to a bookstore and bought a stack of her favorite childhood books, then gave them to the cashier to give away to random children in memory of the daughter to whom she would never again read.

One mother and her four-year-old daughter delivered bouquets of flowers to people in nursing homes in memory of their respective son and brother and of the girl's grandparents.

One person anonymously tended to her ill neighbor's yard in memory of her nephew.

Another bought coffee for the person behind her in line—which set off a ripple of kindnesses that lasted through several more other people as each paid for another.

Regarding her experience of engaging in Kindness Projects, one woman expressed a sentiment I've heard from myriad others: "I am thankful that I can finally see beyond my grief and still be a light in the lives of others, thanks to my son, who showed me how to love."

WHILE GRIEVING the death of someone loved will last a lifetime, if we are able to remain close to our original wound, honestly, being with it and surrendering to it, we can experience a kind of transcendence, a transfiguration. Meaningful moments arise in continuous rhythm. Our hearts are completely, lastingly broken open, turned outward toward others, even others quite unlike us.

We begin to realize oneness in an undeniably personal way.

When we cannot hold in our arms our loved ones who've died, we hold them in our hearts. This is *being with* grief.

When we have been too long in the absence of their song, we turn toward their whispers. This is *surrendering to* grief.

When we cannot look into their eyes, we tender their vision of compassion where it's most needed. This is *doing with* grief.

In every moment without them, we do all we can for others. This is compassion.

Nothing is more mysteriously central to becoming fully human than this process.

43

Through Knowing Suffering

Before you know kindness as the deepest thing inside,
you must know sorrow as the other deepest thing.

—NAOMI SHIHAB NYE

ANNA CALLED ME one October afternoon. She was having a "bad" day.

Anna had come to see me after the death of her four-month-old son, Jared, from SIDS a year earlier. At the time, she'd called herself "beyond suicidal"—a state that she described as so apathetic she couldn't even muster the energy to think about ending her own life.

When she phoned, she was hysterical; I couldn't understand her. When she caught her breath, told me she had been—as we'd discussed—engaging in self-care. We were nearing the anniversary of Jared's death, and she'd done a little shopping and had been eating her favorite meal at her favorite restaurant when a very obviously pregnant woman came in and was seated with her friends near Anna.

She was having a baby shower.

Anna had felt sick.

She described feeling confused and overwhelmed and noticed a surprising anger erupting in her toward the pregnant stranger. Anna told me she'd wanted to turn to the pregnant woman at the baby shower and say, "Save your receipts—*because some babies die!*"

Anna had managed to avoid that outburst, but her mind had been filled with rage and self-loathing. She left her unfinished meal on the table and headed toward the door.

Then she'd paused, taken a deep breath, pulled out a Kindness

Project card, wrote Jared's name on it, and paid the bill for the baby shower, anonymously.

After that, she called me weeping.

We spent almost an hour on the phone discussing how it felt: bittersweet, stinging, honoring, painful, and shameful.

Later that day, I received an email from the MISS Foundation website inquiry form: "My name is Anne, I am a labor and delivery nurse. I was having my baby shower today and someone paid our bill in loving memory of her son Jared Michael. If you know who this lovely person is, would you let her know that she touched all of our lives today, and that when this baby is born she'll know one day that an angel named Jared touched us."

IT IS IN KNOWING SUFFERING, in all its darkest places and with all its most harrowing faces, that we are brought to a place of fierce compassion for others and, perhaps one day, for ourselves.

The road of sorrow is not easy. It is ominous, jarring, and narrow.

We may meet others along the road who offer sustenance: some water, a morsel of food, loving support or guidance, a small candle to light the way, a hand that helps us climb out of a ditch we've fallen into, a patch of shade in which we can shelter from the heat. Such meetings plant seeds.

These seeds of kindness grow one day into our own compassionate care for others.

And, at some point, we ourselves will shade another.

At some times, the turn toward compassionate action unfurls so slowly.

At other times, the calling is more precipitous, a tsunami in response to quakes of fully inhabited grief.

And this is how our world will change.

Those who have deeply suffered understand life in ways other cannot: they know the only way to attain authentic and lasting contentment is to turn our hearts outward in service to those who are suffering as we have suffered.

I am present with life because I am present with death.

I know joy and peace because I am present with grief and suffering.

44

Fierce Compassion

> Since her first grief had brought her fully to birth
> and wakefulness in this world, an unstinting compassion
> had moved in her, like a live stream flowing deep underground
> by which she knew herself and others and the world.
>
> —WENDELL BERRY

I STAY MINDFULLY CLOSE to the sensations of early grief because it is a memorial to the raw pain so ubiquitous in the newly bereaved; I find that my attention to it directs and intensifies my sense of what I think of as *fierce compassion*. Fierce compassion is another artifact of fully inhabited grief.

Compassion, from the root word meaning *to suffer with*, is valued across religions, across time, across cultures. Yet so much of our own modern culture exalts the very antithesis of this by asking us to cure, fix, or cease suffering—which then compounds and exacerbates pain.

ARI, MY FIRSTBORN, was about two years old when I taught him about ants.

He already knew how I felt about animals, how much I love them and that I collected the signatures for the first-ever "Save the Whales" campaign in the 1970s, but he hadn't known how I felt about ants.

We were out walking with his baby brother, Cameron, in the stroller, when I inadvertently stepped on an ant. "Oh no!" I said, and I apologized to the ant. I hadn't seen it even as I had been avoiding stepping on others.

Ari looked at me, stricken. "You killed the ant, Mommy?"

"I did, honey. I accidentally stepped on him."

I could see him think about this for a few long moments.

"We don't step on ants, Mommy," he told me.

"No baby, we don't. We don't kill bugs, and we don't eat animals. We don't want to hurt other creatures if we don't have to."

AS ARI AND HIS SIBLINGS GREW UP, they began to question the value of an ant's life—or any bug that I'd carefully trap under a cup to "re-home" outside.

My friends too had opinions. Some thought I was some sort of "special crazy" to be raising my children with such views.

I would say to my friends: How much more will these kids show compassion toward an animal or another child or another human being if they are taught compassion for a bug? How much more likely will they be to show compassion for another in suffering, one who is wounded and hurt and in need of kindness?

IT IS COMPASSION—suffering with the other—that will help to heal this world.

Our task as humans is to extend compassion to all beings, large and small, like us and unlike us, those in mourning and those in pain— and to extend compassion to our own self.

Compassion toward oneself can manifest in compassion toward others.

And compassion toward others can express compassion toward oneself.

There is no doubt: I am a better person today for having known Cheyenne's beauty.

I am a better person for having loved her.

I am also a better person for having grieved her, even if I continue to wish I'd never had to.

Being the mother of a child who has died is a tragic privilege—one

for which I never asked and certainly never wanted. Yet here I am—
and here you are—unbearably wounded.

It is the bereaved who are awakened from the slumber of self-
satisfaction.

It is the bereaved who can heal our world.

45

The Horse Chemakoh

The first peace, which is the most important, is that
which comes within the souls of people when they realize their relationship, their oneness with the universe and
all its powers, and when they realize that at the center of the universe dwells the Great Spirit, and that this
center is really everywhere, it is within each of us.
—BLACK ELK

I'D ALWAYS WANTED to visit Havasu Falls in the Grand Canyon—
especially since the children and I worked on the puzzle together just
after Chey's death—the puzzle with the missing piece. It was a place
I would bring Cheyenne's love into the world by bearing the shadow
of fierce compassion.

No more than five minutes into the ten-mile hike from the top
of the trail, I came upon a heartrending scene. A horse had fallen to
the ground; he was carrying backpacks, tents, and other supplies that
were tied to a wooden frame mounted to his back. A young man,
wanting the horse to get back on his feet, was abusing him.

I yelled at the man—loudly.

He stopped and looked squarely in my eyes. My heart was pound-
ing; I started to cry.

I imagine it was my tears that scared him; he swiftly took his other
four or five horses back up to the top of the trail.

My friend Nanci and I stayed with this horse as he lay helplessly
on the ground. His head and legs, as they buckled under him, were
bleeding. The horse was limp and terrified—and visibly suffering.

I bent down slowly, reaching out to caress him. He flinched.

I wept, loudly, as others hiked past us.

Some stopped to ask if I was okay.

"This horse . . .! This horse is *hurt*!" I said. "He's been abused!"

But no one could help. Because of our remoteness, there was no cell service; there was no one to call—no police, no rangers.

We removed the horse's heavy packs from his back, and we removed the saddle and wooden frame used to tie the packs, revealing open and bleeding wounds on his back and belly.

He was horrifically emaciated. Vertebrae were protruding through his skin. His hair and skin had abraded away, exposing both hipbones.

I stood up and my head spun. It was one of the most terrible things I have ever seen.

The horse and I looked into each other's eyes, and he allowed me to stroke him. Something overcame me: *I* was that horse many years ago. I, too, had suffered as he was suffering. I, too, knew his fear, despair, and hopelessness. I, too, had stood on death's door.

I promised him that I would help him. And I knew, somehow, that Cheyenne was involved in that moment.

We sat with him for about an hour as he rested on the ground. People continued to pass by, looking up and looking down—but few looking at the horror of the scene.

I plucked scarce grass from the mountainside to offer him. I stroked his head as he rested in my lap. I would not leave him—this precious life, my brother horse, child of the earth, just like me, just like us all.

Over and over again I told him how sorry I was, how sorry I was that humans had done this to him.

"I'm going to get you out of here." I vowed to him. "I'm going to help you. I promise . . ."

When his owner returned, we offered to buy him—twice. The man declined our offers.

There was nothing I could do.

I had to leave without the horse.

I cannot describe this feeling—I was abandoning part of myself on that mountain.

Back at the car, I felt wild and untamed anger in my belly—fierce compassion.

IT WAS NEARLY TWO HOURS before I could get cell service to make calls. I called the forest service, the sheriff, the FBI, local police, animal control; I called legislators, congressional leaders, horse rescues, animal protection groups, superintendents, police chiefs, lawyers. I called colleagues, friends, neighbors.

For two days, not even changing out of my pajamas, I made nearly a hundred phone calls and sent more than a hundred emails.

This animal's life *mattered*—yet I was told repeatedly that there was nothing anyone could do.

But I was not going to stop. I couldn't. I had seen into this animal's soul, and I loved him.

Finally one person, a law enforcement officer, heard my plea and somehow a team of governmental leaders got behind this effort.

SEVEN PHONE CALLS, six emails, and three days later, I got the call.

"Dr. Cacciatore," he said, "how soon can you get here?"

"Really?" I asked, shocked that something was happening. I had been told over and over to "give it up" and that because the horse was on tribal land, I would not be able to help it.

"Yes ma'am . . ." It was around 4 p.m.

For hours, I called trying to locate a horse trailer to rent or borrow. By 10 p.m., with the assistance of a bereaved father I'd once helped, I had a trailer and two heroic volunteers, both men who had also known deep grief and were volunteering to hike into the canyon to rescue the horse. They left for the long drive at midnight and arrived at Hualapai Hilltop at five in the morning. Then they began the sixteen-mile hike to rescue and rehome the horse.

I woke up at 2 praying and waiting—and waiting.

Four hours later, I received a text: "Trail Rider reports that they made it out . . ."

They told me that as they hiked out with the horse—very, very slowly—members of the community nodded at them as they passed by, as if to say, "Yes."

Tourists, shocked by the horse's appearance, thanked the men for saving him.

Meanwhile, I waited.

They brought the horse to my home. He stepped off the trailer, tentative, emaciated, dehydrated, and frightened. And then we saw each other again. The horse, in what seemed like his recognition of the promise to help him, whinnied and walked directly—and specifically—over to me

I named him Chemakoh, a word from the Pima tribe meaning "two souls who came together as one in destiny."

No one knew if he would survive the first few weeks.

THE FIRST FEW DAYS after he arrived home were tenuous. The stallion's wounds were deep—bones eroded through the hair and flesh on his spine and hips, holes worn through to muscle on both sides of his girth.

Even so within weeks we witnessed a dramatic improvement in his health, although we still had a very long road toward his rehabilitation.

I STILL HAVE CHEMAKOH AT MY HOME. He's a therapy horse now and a great teacher for those with whom I work. Somehow he trusts even when he has no reason to risk being hurt again; he loves even though he didn't know love for so many years. He is friendly and affectionate despite the cruelty and horror he's seen; he connects despite years of fear and loneliness. He, too, has had to bear the unbearable.

ALMOST SIX MONTHS AFTER Chemakoh came home, an equine veterinarian—a new one—came to visit him. At the end of the check-up, he handed me an invoice, which include the random birth date he'd assigned to Chemakoh. The date was July 27, 1999—Cheyenne's birthday.

I was stunned. "How did you pick that birth date?" I asked.

He said, "Well, I guess him to be about fifteen, so I picked 1999."

"No, no," I said. "How did you pick July 27?"

"I just picked a date for the visit and put it into the computer."

Tears welled in my eyes.

"Did I do something wrong?" he asked, worried.

"Oh no, no, no," I said. "You did everything perfectly."

A COLLEAGUE SENT ME AN EMAIL not long ago about this horse that would inspire and encourage many broken hearts. He said, "Sometimes, like today, I wake up and wonder if life is pointless, and my heart fills with a foggy numbness. Then you come to mind and I think of what you do and your horse, and then I'm inspired to put my feet on the floor and walk through the day. Thank you for your fierce heart."

We are all connected.

A little drop of love in an ocean of pain can sustain countless beings. It was not compassion alone that let me help that horse: I'd had to manifest ferocity with that compassion, a fierceness that enabled swift and sustained action.

And I'd had to, once again, be willing to be with and surrender again to my own pain—my own grief for the horse, for myself, for the world—before I could act effectively.

46

The Price of Unrealized Grief and Trauma

"Did you see Death go by with my little child?" asked the mother.
"Yes," said the blackthorn bush. "But I shall not tell you which
way he went unless you warm me against your heart—I am
freezing to death; I am stiff with ice."

The mother pressed the blackthorn bush against her heart to
warm it, and the thorns stabbed so deep into her flesh that
great drops of red blood flowed. So warm was the mother's
heart that the blackthorn bush blossomed and put forth green
leaves on that dark winter's night. And it told her the way to go.
—*THE STORY OF A MOTHER*, HANS CHRISTIAN ANDERSEN

"HELLO?" I said.

I heard the raspy voice of an obviously older woman on the other
end of the phone line: "I'm looking for Dr. Joanne Cacciatore."

"This is she."

"Oh, I like you already," she said, laughing. "You answer your own
calls!"

I MET MERINA at my office a few days later, on a beautiful spring day.
The white oleanders were in full blossom, and she was standing outside my office window admiring them when I opened the door to
greet her.

"Oh, my, you're so *young*!" she said—again, laughing. "Are you
sure you're a doctor?"

"Things in the mirror are older than they appear," I told her wryly.

Merina was a retired psychologist and a natural rebel who loved the Oregon coast and the arts and had been "running from grief" since the death of her only daughter Kathy seven years earlier from alcoholism. Merina's anguish was palpable during our meeting, but I noticed again and again that she swiftly changed the subject from her feelings about losing Kathy to more benign topics.

Over time, our relationship deepened. I came to know that she herself was an alcoholic throughout her children's youth, self-medicating an unprocessed childhood trauma of her own. She told me about the many times Kathy had tried to awaken her from a drunken stupor as Merina lay unconscious on the couch. She described the cycle of shame and guilt that fueled her own addictions. She had used not just substances to avoid her pain, but also sexual affairs, travel, even spirituality.

By the time Merina eventually stopped drinking, Kathy had already started, and Merina tried, time after time, to save Kathy from her own path of alcoholism and addiction. By the time Kathy was in her early forties, she'd had two children and was "a full-blown alcoholic just like her mother . . . repeating the only thing she knew." At age forty-three, Kathy was hospitalized for severe physical illnesses arising from her alcohol abuse.

While in the hospital, Kathy had asked Merina, "Mom, am I going to die?"

Merina assured her she would not and promised everything would be okay.

Two days later, Kathy died.

KATHY'S DEATH was too much for Merina to bear—and so she didn't bear it.

She withdrew from family and friends. She didn't talk about Kathy's death, or Kathy at all, in anything but superficialities. And she lost her passion for life.

By the time Merina found me, although she wasn't using substances, her avoidance was making her physically ill and completely disconnected.

We worked together for three years, and Merina was diligent. She created timelines of her life, identifying events that she felt contributed to her own intolerance of emotions. She explored her own mother's traumatic grief and the generations of family losses that she came to realize had set herself up for needing to always "be five feet outside" her own body. She came to understand that the harm she'd brought forth was the result of generations of unspoken, unprocessed pain. Her parent's suffering, in particular, had become her own; she'd internalized it. Add to that her own childhood trauma and there was no way she could cope with the inner turmoil alone. Her initial pain was exacerbated by her own evasions and those of her mother. It was a feedback loop of dysfunction from which she did not know how to extricate herself.

Over time, she learned to trust me, trust us—and to trust her grief.

She started to reconnect with friends using our own healthy relationship as a model. She also began to reach out to her three surviving sons, meaningfully rebuilding those relationships. And Merina also gradually reconnected with her own real emotions and was able to tell Kathy's story while crying and "not feeling the least bit of shame for it." And she kept an emotion journal that would document all three years of our time together.

She noticed that as her heart opened and softened she'd begun to see all the suffering in the world as her own. She reported her internal judging voice had "left the building like Elvis." Her passion for life returned.

ONE DAY Merina came into my office looking solemn and said, "You know, at one point, I would have been overjoyed to tell people this. But now that I've been working with you, I'm not so sure."

I waited.

"I'm dying," she said. "I have cancer, and I'm dying. They say six to nine months."

Tears came, for us both.

My heart ached—I had come to love Merina and I knew her death would hurt me deeply.

We continued our work together, our focus shifting between the grief she felt over Kathy's death and practical preparation for her own inevitable mortality—which she faced with a grace I'd rarely witnessed.

We ate many "possibly last" meals together.

I helped her give away her owl totems and favorite hats and scarves to friends.

"It's okay now," she told me, one week before she died. "It's not okay that Kathy died before me, but to be surrounded by so much love has been amazing and I'm so grateful."

She wanted three people there when she died, and I was one of them. We chose her death song, "Fear Not" by State of Grace. We picked the flowers she wanted at her bedside. She prearranged her own cremation.

She wanted to die wearing her favorite purple hat.

She gave me a letter, instructing me to read it after her death. "Without you," she'd written, "I would not be dying in peace. What a gift you have given me. I love you, thank you—and I'll see you again."

I still miss Merina.

47

Transgenerational Grief

After all, when a stone is dropped into a pond, the water continues quivering even after the stone has sunk to the bottom.

—ARTHUR GOLDEN

ROSE AND NICOLA—my mother's parents—were uneducated and exceedingly poor Sicilians who lived in a tiny cramped apartment in Palermo. She was a seamstress, and he was a barber who loved to play the mandolin. She was strict, direct, and detached; he was phlegmatic, withdrawn, and distant. They had three children: Mary, Josephine, and Salvatore. Josephine was my mother.

Both Rose and Nicola spoke only broken English, so I knew them primarily through my mother's interpretation. I was close to neither.

Times were hard in Sicily during the early twentieth century: child death was common; infant death, rampant. Communicable illness, resource scarcity, traumatic births, and malnutrition all held open the door for death. Without mercy, sometimes death took out entire families.

I WAS CLEANING OUT old boxes of family photographs just two weeks before my grandmother's death, when she was seventy-nine and I was twenty-five. Photo after photo had edges worn from handling, some with faces faded beyond recognition. I stumbled on a photo of a baby on a horse.

"Who's this?" I asked Rose.

She took the photo and looked at it.

"That's Josephine," she said.

"Josephine? That doesn't look like my mom."

"Oh no," she said, "that was the *first* Josephine."

"What do you mean 'the first Josephine'?"

In her strong Italian accent she tried to explain that her first baby, who had also been named Josephine, died at a year old, of pneumonia, she thought.

"So my mom is the second Josephine, named after the first?"

"No," Rose said.

She went on to explain that she had a *second* baby the next year, very soon after the first Josephine died. She'd named that second baby Josephine too. The second Josephine lived for six months and died in her sleep.

How could I not have known this? Why hadn't anyone told me?

My grandmother's third baby, whom she named Mary, lived.

Her fourth, she named Josephine again. My mother was the third Josephine.

My mother's parents had had five children. Five, not three: Josephine, Josephine, Mary, Josephine, and Salvatore.

She had never spoken of grief, never expressed it, but I knew it was there buried in her soul.

My grandmother was not a warm person. She was muted, beige, and lacked zest for life. I don't know if she was always that way, but I suspect not. Losing two beloved children—and never fully grieving for them—will change a person. And those changes pervade generations.

REPRESSED GRIEF ravages individuals and dismantles families; its tragic effects seep like groundwater into communities and societies. And the emotional economics of grief denied its rightful place are grim.

The century-long American Indian genocide eradicated entire cultures; it is a historical abomination that few outside of tribal people and their governments want to remember, acknowledge, or feel—let alone recompense.

Transgenerational trauma, also called historical trauma, is real and exceedingly potent. It can be seen in family systems and in cultural systems.

The deep psychological wounds and near obliteration of tribes; the killing of countless native children and adults; the subjugation, enslavement, torture, oppression, involuntary diaspora, and kidnapping of children from their families and tribes are a calamitous trauma that has been burned into the minds and hearts of those who suffered at the hands of European occupiers and their descendants.

Dr. Maria Yellow Horse Brave Heart identified the effects of this kind of trauma in her work. It causes such things as traumatic stress, depressive symptoms, exceedingly high premature mortality, poor physical health, alcohol abuse, domestic violence against women and children, and even animal abuse. These things interconnect in a dangerous web of enduring risk, perpetuating the cycle of suffering once only inflicted by outsiders.

She identified what she calls six phases of unresolved historical trauma and grief, the first of which is "No time for grief."

There is not time enough to grieve when such horrors are vast, systemic, en masse, and unrelenting—so grief is circumvented at a heavy cost.

Yet as we've seen again and again, grief demands to be seen. It demands to be heard. It demands a channel of expression. Suppressed, deflected, silenced, and internalized traumatic grief bursts forth in myriad damaging ways. This is true for individuals, and for families, and for cultures.

The effects of "no time for grief"—of denying grief's demands—are addictions, abuse, and violence, often against the vulnerable: children, women, the elderly, and animals.

The alternative to repressing grief is to fully inhabit it.

When we have learned to fully inhabit our grief, we awaken to the suffering in others. We recognize harm in all relations, human-to-human, human-to-child, human-to-animal, child-to-animal. And then, having awakened to our own suffering and the suffering of others, we can begin to take actions, when and where we can, that serve to diminish suffering rather than amplify it.

We must reach out to others less fortunate and show compassion, because to receive compassion, even if over time and slowly, is to know compassion. And to know compassion, even if from ourselves, is to be able to show compassion.

We cannot give what we've never received.

48

Grief Broth

Time past and time future
What might have been and what has been
Point to one end, which is always present.

—T.S. ELIOT

I WAS COOKING vegetable soup one day for a friend.

I put cilantro, one of my favorite herbs, in the recipe. Unfortunately, she was one of those people for whom its taste is aversive.

I picked out the cilantro leaves, but it didn't matter for her. The taste of the cilantro had merged with the carrots, celery, broccoli, kale, tomatoes, sea salt, and barley—every flavor synthesized into one broth. It couldn't be removed, isolated, or neutralized.

Grief is this way too.

I ADOPTED A STRAY DOG, a brindled English mastiff, from a shelter on a fall day just before the year's first snowfall. I named her Maggie, and called her Mags. When I first met her, she was frail, malnourished. She should have weighed almost two hundred pounds; instead she weighed sixty-five. She walked with her back end curled nearly under her body, her lanky tail tucked between her front and rear legs. She was terrified.

I was terrified too—because I knew I was going to try to save her from the horrors that other humans had foisted on her. For two weeks, day and night, I cleared my calendar and stayed with her, caring for her—taxiing her back and forth to emergency clinics and vets more times than I can count, cleaning up vomit, staying up to comfort her fears all through many nights, cooking five different meals for her until she would accept a mere bite or two of nourishment.

It turned out Mags had been so starved by her previous owners that she'd eaten a corncob, which had lodged in her small intestines. She underwent surgery to have it removed. Coming home after that, she immediately began to eat again and drink.

And her health gradually improved. No matter what discomfort she endured, she would sit next to me, trusting me, already loving me.

I took her on four short walks every day. She and Chemakoh liked each other very much. I think Mags regarded him as a big dog, and he seemed to look at her as a very small horse.

On the third day after the surgery, she became very sick. Her breathing was labored and rattled. An X-ray at the vet's emergency room showed that her lung had collapsed.

She would likely not survive, the doctor told me. I wept. Mags sat on the X-ray table draped in her blanket. We would continue to try to save her—oxygen, fluids, IV antibiotics—but her veins would not sustain the IV.

Mags died early in the morning at home in her bed, her frail bones held together only by skin. My heart was shattered.

I was unhinged—by her death but also by the deaths of both my parents months before, by the death of my daughter years ago.

I was wrecked.

I SPENT MOST OF THE NEXT TWO DAYS WEEPING. That sweet dog had worked her way into my heart in a very big way.

I was saddened and angry with the humans who had failed her— and the humans who, every day all around the world, fail the children and animals and elderly and anyone vulnerable who are in need of compassion and kindness but who do not receive such love.

I just could not stop crying. I'd had so many other, arguably more significant and painful, losses. Why was this one affecting me in what seemed to be a disproportionate way?

Then I thought about the cilantro.

Mags's death was one ingredient in a big bowl of grief broth.

The pain of losing her blended with grief for Cheyenne and for my parents and Elisabeth and Terri and all my dead people. This was about them all.

Grief is synergistic, the whole growing greater than the sum of the individual parts.

This realization reminded me to stop questioning and doubting the waves of grief that were hitting me and just allow my emotions to be what they were.

TWO DAYS LATER, I had an appointment I had to keep, so I very reluctantly made myself presentable and drove to it—down the same road that took me to the vet, the same road I'd driven so many times with Mags.

I cried.

I had feelings of panic and distress.

I cried more.

I asked, in my head, the familiar existential questions: *What happens when we die? What happens when animals die? Did Mags feel my love? Did I do enough? Is Mags with Cheyenne?*

A white Lexus pulled in front of me—a large object was moving back and forth in the back seat. Suddenly, a head popped out the back window. I thought I was seeing Mags.

Now first, the English mastiff is not a commonly owned breed. A brindle mastiff is even rarer. I pulled closer to the car with skeptical curiosity and tried (dangerously) to take some photographs with my phone.

The Lexus turned into a nearby neighborhood, and I followed it, thinking I'd either gone mad or was now an official dog-stalker.

The car turned up a driveway. I parked on the street and waited.

The driver exited his vehicle as I stood on the street in front of his house.

"I'm so sorry to follow you," I said to him, "and I'm not crazy—really. But . . . is that an English mastiff?"

"Yes," he said carefully.

"Brindle?"

"Yes, she's a brindle," he said.

"Oh my gosh, a *girl* too?!"

I think at this point the man was getting frightened—or at least concerned.

"Um, well, you see, my dog just died. I tried to save her. And she just died, and I'm so sad, and I was just wondering about souls and dogs," I babbled and stumbled. "Please, can I just see your dog?"

"Of course," he said.

She jumped out of the car playfully. She looked just like Mags, her face, coloring, and even her disposition. But she was obviously healthy and hadn't been abused. I bent over and stroked her. The man told me her name was Cleopatra.

I explained more of the story to this kind and generous man I had stalked.

I showed him Mags's photos, and he was shocked by her condition. I told him how much I had wanted Mags to make it and how much she and Cleopatra resembled each other. I told him about the sleepless nights and vomit and medications and force-feedings and cuddles. I told him how very happy I was that I had gotten to meet his Cleopatra in this moment, how *very* much I had needed this.

He listened sympathetically. "I really admire you for trying to save her," he said. "Not everyone would have done what you did for her. Thank you."

Then he reached out his hand and said, "What's your name?"

"I'm Joanne, but my friends call me Jojo," I answered with grateful tears in my eyes.

"Jojo, it's nice to meet you," he replied. "My name is Cheyenne."

Why did I feel such pain when Mags died?

Because grief is like broth. Because Cheyenne died. And my parents died. And my friends died. And because I have known suffering and Mags knew suffering. The flavors of all these griefs merged and became one flavor.

Grief transforms from the individual into the collective.

49

The Darkness Has Its Gifts

No one is as capable of gratitude as one
who has emerged from the kingdom of night.

—ELIE WIESEL

KELLI was an introverted, confident, self-made woman who married her first love and worked in the nonprofit arts. After seventeen years together, she and her husband, Richard, suffered the tragic death during birth of their firstborn daughter, Madeleine.

Kelli not only suffered the loss of her only child but experienced additional trauma at the hands of a compassionless medical system. This infused such despair into her already existing traumatic grief that she felt unsafe in the world and began to withdraw into a cocoon of self-protection.

She came to me several years after Madeleine's death—afraid she would die without being fully connected to both of her daughters— her living child Alaina as well as Madeleine.

Kelli's physical health was in rapid decline, and her personality had changed significantly since losing Madeleine. She mistrusted herself. She mistrusted others. Her sense of competency had dissolved. Kelli was so terrified of grief, of being "sucked into the abyss of pain," that she avoided allowing herself to feel anything at all. And in order to do that, she'd had to lock away Madeleine's memory.

Kelli had very little experience with grief before Madeleine's death. And after it, she believed that in order to be healthy and functional, and to be a good mother to her second-born child, she needed to avoid grief. So she expended a great deal of energy trying not to think about

Madeleine. Kelli didn't talk about her. She didn't look at photographs. She "distracted as much as possible" and tried to protect herself from painful emotions, terrified that the heaviness of grief would drag her into depression.

Unable to acknowledge Madeleine and her grief, she felt increasingly disconnected, numb, isolated, broken. She said she felt stuck, "like a prisoner inside the walls I created. I hated the new me—seemingly okay on the outside, lifeless and empty inside. On a dead-end path."

She wanted to "start over" and so had reached out to me.

OUR WORK TOGETHER focused on the ways in which she could remain connected to Madeleine. Turning toward her grief, Kelli began to experience the intense feelings that she'd been so sternly avoiding. She looked at Madeleine's pictures again. She began to trust her relationship with me and Madeleine's place in our relationship.

Kelli described the unfolding of this work as "a long and tortuous time" during which she often felt sick and anxious. And she said she felt "deep, intense pain that seemed like it would never end." It's easy to see why a person would seek relief from such angst, but Kelli's bravery pushed her to continue with the work.

She wrote,

I felt incompetent for not being more in touch with my feelings. I felt like a failure at my job, at home, with my grief. I felt weak for being so unhappy and ignorant for not being able to get through this better. Unsure if I was headed down another doomed path, I allowed myself to feel whatever came up for as long as I needed. It took an exceptionally long time, and it felt like taking several—very painful—steps backwards. In reality, it's what I needed to do. Eventually, grief became less torturous and more natural. I stopped focusing on where I should be in my grief and just focused on my love for Madeleine. It reconnected me to my true feelings for my daughter. Looking back, I don't think

I would have ever experienced true joy and love again had I not fully experienced the pain so deeply and for so long.

Grieving Madeleine has been a painfully slow and often daunting process for Kelli. She eventually gave herself over to the grief, surrendering space for Madeleine in a way that held, and ennobled, meaning for her in grief.

One day, I received this email from her:

> **Dr. Jo,**
> You know how you talk about beauty and pain coexisting? This has been an exceptionally hard concept for me to grasp since my daughter died. On a theoretical level, I get it. It makes sense. I have tried very hard to believe it. In reality, I haven't felt it. Everything that was beautiful stopped that day. Music, art, literature, nature, people, philosophy—everything important changed on such a grand scale, I thought I would never again experience anything but a diminished reality of what I used to love. Only recently have I begun to truly feel that beauty still exists, and perhaps more intensely. What I didn't realize is that beauty only exists now because I had to fully experience the pain first, and only the pain, for as long as I needed to. Pretty sure this is what you've been saying all along, but being the existentialist that I am, I had to experience it.
>
> You have been the only one who didn't try to convince me that what I felt, or didn't feel, following her death was wrong. And, you didn't rush me.
>
> And you didn't bullshit me. For that, I will always be grateful.

Kelli gradually discovered that her grief, lived openly, held a mysterious conciliatory power.

Today, her grief has been recast into *doing with*, compassionate action, through her work as the executive director of the MISS Foundation, helping other parents who have lost a child.

50

What I Know

The more difficult the journey,
the greater the depth of purification.
—*SEVEN YEARS IN TIBET*

I FOUND MYSELF cleaning out the contents of an old drawer. I came across a faded yellow Post-it note written by my then-seven-year-old son:

> This Is to You Mom.
> I Love You More Than Life Itself.
> You Are The Best Mom Ever
> And When I Say Ever I Mean EVER !!!

My youngest, Josh, had written me this, folded into a tiny square that contained a crumpled photograph of us. I took the sweet note and put it into a large storage box, my place for exceptional memories that holds cherished reminders of my children's childhood.

I acknowledge that I, perhaps, tend to save more of these mementos than some mothers. I hoard memories like a bereaved mother because I know some painfully learned truths.

I know life is fleeting, and sometimes children die.

And I know that life promises us nothing.

I know that forgiveness does not come easily in grief, especially toward myself.

I know that no drink, no pill, no religion, and no book can save me from suffering.

I know that people we love can and do die and that no one is exempt.

I know that control is an illusion.

I know that one day, one year, ten years, twenty years, and fifty years is never enough time with those we love.

I know that there is nothing we can trade, nothing we can barter, nothing we can give to negotiate our loved ones back to life—not even offering ourselves in their place.

And I know the secret that life goes on, but it's never the same.

WHEN I REMAIN CONSCIOUS of my susceptibility to suffering, I notice the constant hum of fear, a rumble of insatiable terror, and I remind myself how normal it is to be afraid to lose again, to want some type of guarantee or protection against more trauma and grief.

And, I know this is unattainable.

We are all connected by suffering and loss, and unless we manage to avoid love, we will not avoid grief.

Your tears are not only your tears; my tears are not only my tears.

Imagine that the tears we shed will make their way into a creek near our homes, which leads to the river miles away, which flows into the great ocean of sorrow. Other creeks and other rivers have carried to the same ocean the sorrows of many other mothers and fathers and sisters and brothers and grandparents and lovers and spouses and friends and aunts and uncles and neighbors and strangers who have also grieved, who have also deeply mourned.

The myth of separateness is an illusion to keep us safe from vulnerability; separateness is a mirage that stifles realization of our connectedness.

The great ocean of sorrow merges many to one, the knowing into the unknown, the wisdom into the wonder, and the questions into the great mystery—throughout history and across geography and beyond culture.

Every tear you shed and all the countless tears shed by myriad others throughout time and space have become drops in the vast oceanic story of loving and grieving.

THE UNNECESSARY AGONY born from our disconnected feelings and lack of compassion for ourselves and others has been told in story after story. Over and over, we see the grave consequences of a grief not brought forth, when it is denied, avoided, repressed—when our biographies of loss are locked up and hidden away.

Losing our beloved brings a pain unlike any other—and this pain is legitimately ours.

Being with grief is terrifyingly painful, yet when we live our grief honestly, it has the mysterious power to deepen the meaning of our lives.

This is the gift-curse of grief.

When we come to deeply *be with* the finitude of our lives, and the lives of those we love, our appreciation for everything is deepened.

We touch a vibrancy, a richness—and we begin to wake up.

This other person we love could die at any time.

And we too will die.

We realize that every moment is a secret cache.

Each breath is an offering.

And every increment of time is irreplaceable.

The only thing for which life offers even a fleeting guarantee is this moment—right here and right now. This is all we have, all we ever have.

It is both absolving and terrifying.

Epilogue

Whosoever survives the test must tell his story.
That is his duty.
—ELIE WIESEL

IT WAS PITCH BLACK OUTSIDE, and I was sitting on the train returning from my East Coast speaking tour as we made our way through the Cibola National Forest in New Mexico.

I was in line waiting to be seated in the dining car next to a middle-aged woman and her daughter. Such trains as the one I was on seat tables of four people for meals. We were at the end of the line, so at the table it was just the three of us.

We made small talk. I grumbled about being sick of the same vegan burger for breakfast, lunch, and dinner. They made small talk about siblings and growing their own food. They asked where I got on this train.

Then, as had happened repeatedly on this trip, the conversation took a familiar, tentative turn when she asked why I was on the train. I told her.

"Oh my gosh," she said, "traumatic death? Wow." She looked at her daughter. "My husband just died two years ago. He was diagnosed with cancer and died nineteen days later." She talked about her grief, their grief, and how her faith that she would see him again helped her and her children. Her daughter, who I now knew was twenty-two years old, smiled sweetly at her mother, and I found myself wondering if Cheyenne, who would have been nearly twenty-two years old herself, would smile like that at me if she were alive.

The woman asked me directly if I had lost someone and if that was the impetus for my work. Strangely, in all the encounters with others for the past six weeks, no one had put this question to me.

I momentarily debated how to answer—this hardly felt like cheerful dinner conversation. Still, I replied, but only briefly. "I lost a child a long time ago."

"I hope its okay to ask. Is the child you lost your firstborn?"

"No," I said, "my daughter who died was number four of five."

"Oh gosh. This one too," she said, pointing to her daughter sitting with us. "Cheyenne is my fourth of five children."

And now I knew why I *really* liked them and why I sat there for my last meal on this particular journey.

Later, I went back to my cabin and I cried.

Acknowledgments

THIS BOOK has been shaped by the experts, the mourners themselves. Based on two decades of personal experience, direct practice, and research, I explore with you unedited stories of grief and love. Some of the names have been changed while others, where anonymity was not desired, have not. I stand in eternal gratitude to Joe, Oz, Kelli and her Madeleine, Dave, Karla and her Theo, Mirabai and her Jenny, Maya and her Ronan, Genki and Genmitsu, Dr. Robert Stolorow and his Emily, Dr. John and Nikki DeFrain, Dr. Gabor Maté, Dr. Peter Barr, Dr. Geoff Warburton, my stand-in-mom Dr. Elisabeth Kübler-Ross, my colleagues at Arizona State University, especially Drs. Paz Zorita and Cindy Lietz, Dr. Ruth Fretts, Dr. Ramsey Eric Ramsey, Dr. Robert Neimeyer, Dr. Kenneth Doka, Dr. Jerome Wakefield, Dr. Allen Frances, Dr. Irvin Yalom, and all my friends who have supported my work over the past decades.

I want to express my shared grief and gratitude to the parents, spouses, children, and others who allowed me to tell their stories of loss and to the tens of thousands of bereaved families with whom I've worked over the past decades. I am humbled to have been entrusted with this most important part of their lives.

I am deeply grateful, in *gassho*, to Josh Bartok, my editor, for believing in the importance of my work and encouraging me to write this book. And finally, to my beautiful children, Arman, Cameron, Stevie Jo, Cheyenne, and Joshua: thank you for supporting my work, even when it took time away from family. Thank you for seeing the tremendous need in communities around the world and for sacrificing a "normal family life" to help so many others. I love you more than words can express.

About the Author

DR. JOANNE CACCIATORE has a fourfold relationship with bereavement. She is herself a bereaved mother: her newborn daughter died on July 27, 1994, and that single tragic moment catapulted her unwillingly onto the reluctant path of traumatic grief. For more than two decades, she's devoted herself to direct practice with grief, helping traumatically bereaved people on six continents. She's also been researching and writing about grief for more than a decade in her role as associate professor at Arizona State University and director of the Graduate Certificate in Trauma and Bereavement program there. And, in addition, she's the founder of an international nongovernmental organization, the MISS Foundation, dedicated to providing multiple forms of support to families experiencing the death of a child at any age and from any cause, and since 1996 has directed the foundation's family services and clinical education programs.

Cacciatore is an ordained Zen priest, affiliated with Zen Garland and its child bereavement center outside of New York City. She is in the process of building Selah House, a "care-farm" and respite center for the traumatically bereaved, just outside Sedona, Arizona. The care-farm will offer a therapeutic community that focuses on reconnecting with self, others, and nature in the aftermath of loss through gardening, meditation, yoga, group work, animals, and other non-medicalized approaches. All the animals at the care-farm will have been rescued from abuse and neglect.

She is an acclaimed public speaker and provides expert consulting and witness services in the area of traumatic loss. Her research has been published in peer-reviewed journals such as *The Lancet*, *Social Work and Healthcare*, and *Death Studies*, among others.

She received her PhD from the University of Nebraska-Lincoln and her master's and bachelor's degrees in psychology from Arizona State University. Her work has been featured in major media sources such as *People* and *Newsweek* magazines, the *New York Times*, the *Boston Globe*, CNN, National Public Radio, and the *Los Angeles Times*. She has been the recipient of many regional and national awards for her empathic work and service to people suffering traumatic grief.

She travels quite often but spends most of her time in Sedona, Arizona, with her family and three rescue dogs. She also has three horses that are part of her *Rescue Horses Rescue People* equine therapy program.

She's also the author of *Grieving Is Loving: Compassionate Words for Bearing the Unbearable*.

What to Read Next from Wisdom Publications

Grieving Is Loving
Compassionate Words for Bearing the Unbearable
Joanne Cacciatore

"*Grieving Is Loving* is a wise, moving, and compassionate book. Reading it brought tears to my eyes as it reminded me of the loss of loved ones thirty and forty-five years ago. Not only should its message be read and internalized by those suffering the loss of a beloved, but also by those with friends who have lost or are likely to lose someone in the future—in other words, by everyone."
—Irving Kirsch, PhD, Harvard Medical School, University of Connecticut, University of Hull, author of *The Emperor's New Drugs: Exploding the Antidepressant Myth*

A Buddhist Grief Observed
Guy Newland

"Guy Newland's *A Buddhist Grief Observed* is a powerful reflection on his experience of losing his wife to cancer . . . an extraordinary book."—*Buddhadharma*

Lessons from the Dying
Rodney Smith

"This is a valuable book of practice, stories, and meditations."
—Jack Kornfield, author of *A Path with Heart*

Awake at the Bedside
Contemplative Teachings on Palliative and End-of-Life Care
Koshin Paley Ellison and Matt Weingast
Foreword by His Holiness the Karmapa, Ogyen Trinley Dorje

"The greatest degree of inner tranquility comes from the development of love and compassion. The more we care for the happiness of others, the greater is our own sense of well-being. Cultivating a close, warmhearted feeling for others automatically puts the mind at ease. It is the ultimate source of success in life. *Awake at the Bedside* supports this development of love and compassion."
—His Holiness the Dalai Lama

Zen Cancer Wisdom
Tips for Making Each Day Better
Daju Suzanne Friedman

"This book has become one of my most valuable resources. It's a rich and comprehensive guide to opening our minds to our life as it is and for soothing our struggling bodies."
—Toni Bernhard, author of *How to Be Sick*

Mindful Therapy
A Guide for Therapists and Helping Professionals
Thomas Bien

"An elegant guide for both novice and veteran therapists alike."
—Mark Brady, PhD, editor of *The Wisdom of Listening*

Saying Yes to Life
(Even the Hard Parts)
Ezra Bayda and Josh Bartok
Foreword by Thomas Moore

"Astonishing."—*Spirituality & Health*

Wisdom

About Wisdom Publications

Wisdom Publications is the leading publisher of classic and contemporary Buddhist books and practical works on mindfulness. To learn more about us or to explore our other books, please visit our website at wisdomexperience.org or contact us at the address below.

Wisdom Publications
132 Perry Street
New York, NY 10014 USA

We are a 501(c)(3) organization, and donations in support of our mission are tax deductible.

Wisdom Publications is affiliated with the Foundation for the Preservation of the Mahayana Tradition (FPMT).

Thank you for buying this book!

Let Joanne Cacciatore continue to guide you along your path of grief in her Wisdom Academy online course:

wisdomexperience.org/courses/bearing-unbearable/